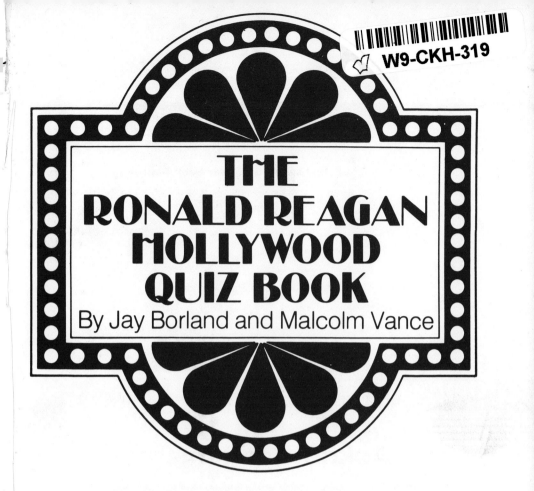

THE RONALD REAGAN HOLLYWOOD QUIZ BOOK

By Jay Borland and Malcolm Vance

NEW YORK

Produced and Packaged: David M. Cohn Publishing, Inc.
Graphics: A Good Thing, Inc.
Jacket Design: Beverly Haw
Composition: Sandcastle
Editorial and Production Services: Cobb-Dunlop, Inc.

Acknowledgements

Dedicated to Roberta Healey Gobin and Joe and Madeline Borland

The authors' special thanks to the following friends who helped along the way (in alphabetical order, so they will remain friends): Judie Annino, Dorothy Chowinski, Dolores Elliott, Hal Haskell, Noreen Kremer, Rhoda Lamson, George Modesta, Rose Sardow, and last, but hardly least, Lewis Chambers, our agent.

PHOTO CREDITS: FROM THE COLLECTION OF THE AUTHOR: p.8(right); p.9(top); p.13; p.15; p.19; p.21; p.23(top); p.25; p.35; p.37; p.45; p.47; p.49(both); p.51; p.55(bottom); p.57; p.59; p.64; p.67(bottom); p.69; p.71(both); p.73; p.75; p.77; p.79; p.85; p.89(both); p.97; p.99; p.101; p.103; p.105; p.108; p.109; p.113(both); p.115; p.116; p.117(both). FROM PENGUIN PHOTOS: p.8(left); p.9(bottom); p.12; p.15(top&bottom); p.17(both); p.23(bottom); p.29(both); p.p.31; p.33; p.41(both); p.43; p.53(both); p.55(top); p.61; p.63; p.65(all); p.67(top left & right); p.94(both); p.95.

Contents

Introduction

Even if actor Ronald Reagan had not gone on to become a two-term governor of California and President of the United States, his Hollywood career would be well worth recounting. While he never became a superstar of Errol Flynn's or Clark Gable's magnitude, Ronald Reagan spent almost three decades in show business, during which time he worked in 55 films, served six consecutive terms as president of the Screen Actors Guild, testified before the House on Un-American Activities Committee, traveled around the country for General Electric, gave speeches and appeared on television as that company's chief host and spokesperson, hosted another popular TV series and met scores of important politicians and business people, to say nothing of almost everyone of any note in Hollywood.

Ronald Reagan's film career commenced in 1937 and ended in 1964. During those 27 years, he worked in films (and almost invariably became friends) with such luminaries as Errol Flynn, Ann Sheridan, Humphrey Bogart, Bette Davis, PatO'Brien, Jimmy Cagney, Dick Powell, George Murphy, Virginia Mayo, Olivia de Havilland, Patricia Neal, Ginger Rogers, Doris Day and heavyweight champion Joe Louis - to name just a few! Oh yes, Ronald Reagan also worked in films with Jane Wyman, who became his first wife, and later appeared in a 1957 film with a lovely actress who still had the screen name of Nancy Davis, although she was already Mrs. Ronald Reagan in real-life.

Ronald Reagan's Hollywood friends also included an array of stars with whom he never appeared on the silver screen. Among the closest of those now deceased were John Wayne, Robert Taylor and Jack Benny. Among Ronald Reagan's closest living Hollywood friends are Jimmy Stewart, Roy Rogers, William Holden, Dean Martin and Frank Sinatra.

This quizbook is intended as a tribute not only to former actor Ronald Reagan, but to all of his many Hollywood friends and film co-workers. For one of them, Joe Louis, perhaps the greatest heavyweight champion of all time and certainly one of the finest humans to ever grace the prize ring, President Reagan ordered a hero's burial in Arlington National Cemetery.

THE RONALD REAGAN ONWARD-AND-UPWARD QUIZ

(Score five points for each correct answer.)

1. While in Iowa, the horse-loving Reagan joined a certain U.S. Reserve unit that is now a thing of the past. What unit?
2. Thus began Ronald Reagan's military career. What year was it?
3. Because of his myopia, Ronald Reagan had to cheat to pass the Army eye test. True or False?
4. While working as a sports announcer, Ronald Reagan editorialized against the exclusion of blacks from major league baseball. True or False?
5. Reagan's sportscasting duties took him every year out to Catalina Island, off the California coast, where he covered the spring training of a midwestern baseball team. What team?
6. In 1937 Reagan was introduced to a Hollywood agent by an actress/singer whom he had met back in Davenport. What was her name?
7. The agent introduced Reagan to Max Arnow, a casting director at a major Hollywood studio. Which studio?
8. What kind of test was Reagan given at the studio?
9. Reagan signed a contract with the studio. For how many years was it?
10. One reason the studio signed Reagan was the similarity of his voice to Ross Alexander's, an actor who had died prematurely. How had he died?
11. Under the auspices of Bernie Foy, the studio's executive of B films, Reagan was immediately put into a picture. What was it?
12. Ronnie Reagan got along famously with Bernie Foy, who was one of seven siblings. Who was Bernie Foy's celebrated vaudevillian father?
13. Incidentally, who later portrayed Bernie Foy's famous father on film?
14. In 1938 and 1939 Ronald Reagan worked in approximately approximately 30 percent of all the films he would make in his career. How many films did Reagan make in 1938 and 1939?

15. Although most of his pictures in 1938 belonged in the B category, at least one - <u>Brother Rat</u> - was and still is a first-class film. Whom did he get to know on that set who would play a major role in his real life?

16. Reagan and his first wife were married on January 26, 1940, at the Wee Kirk Heather Church in a celebrated Los Angeles cemetery. What cemetery?

17. What Hollywood <u>grande dame</u> and gossip columnist (whom an irreverent Marlon Brando would refer to years later as the "fat one") gave a wedding reception for Ronald Reagan and his radiant bride?

18. Ronald and Jane's first child, Maureen Elizabeth, was born on January 27, 1941, which also happened to be the 27th birthday of one of Maureen's parents. Which one?

19. In what year did the Reagans adopt a boy whom they named Michael Edward?

20. On June 26, 1947, a Reagan daughter was born four months prematurely. What happened to her?

Mrs. Nelle Wilson Reagan and son,
Ronald Wilson Reagan.

Fan magazine photo of Ronald Reagan.

Ronald Reagan with daughter Maureen.

Publicity photo of the young film star with
"Tarbaby", one of his favorite horses.

RONALD REAGAN WAR YEARS QUIZ

(Score five points for each correct answer.)

Although America didn't enter World War II until the Japanese attacked Peal Harbor on December 7, 1941, the war commenced when Germany invaded Poland on September 1, 1939.

1. Ronald Reagan has always been a good family man. He brought his parents out to Hollywood not long after his arrival there. Although his father suffered from a heart condition that precluded regular work, he was given a job by his actor son. What type of job?
2. In 1940 Reagan persuaded Warner Bros. to let him play George Gipp in Knute Rockne-All American. Warner Bros. had at first been reluctant to cast Reagan in that role because it felt that despite his fine physique he somehow did not look like a ...Like a what?
3. Speaking of Reagan's fine physique, after his appearance in Knute Rockne-All American, the art students in a University of Southern California sculpture class asked him to pose for them in a bathing suit-they said he had the body of a Greek god. Which Greek god?
4. The affable Reagan obliged the students, posing in a bathing suit and holding a football. Then, as now, he stood six-one and weighed in the neighborhood of a very trim 180. His chest was 41 inches. What size was his waist?
5. His next film after Knute Rockne was Tugboat Annie Sails Again. What blood relative of Ronnie's had a small part in that film?
6. Following Tugboat Annie, he played George Armstrong Custer in Santa Fe Trail, a handsomely mounted historical film with an all-star cast that included perhaps the handsomest man in Hollywood, whom Reagan called "a strange person, terribly unsure of himself and needlessly so. He was a beautiful piece of machinery, likable, with great charm, and yet convinced he lacked ability." Who was he?
7. Reagan really hit the big time when Warner Bros. gave him a strong supporting role in Kings Row,

probably the best picture in which he ever appeared and certainly the one in which he gave his best performance. For perhaps the first and last time in his screen career, Reagan played a role that was psychologically draining, one that obliged him to plumb the depths of his emotions. After Kings Row, his agent managed to triple Reagan's salary, making it more than $3,000 a week. Who was his agent?

8. Reagan was not able to capitalize on Kings Row. After that picture he made two undistinguished films—Juke Girl and Desperate Journey—before leaving the U.S. Cavalry Reserve and joining the regular U.S. Army. He entered the latter with the same rank he had held in the former. What rank was that?

9. The myopia that had almost kept him out of the Cavalry Reserves almost kept him out of the regular Army as well. What had Reagan worn for many years in lieu of eye glasses?

10. After reporting to San Francisco's Fort Dixon (shades of his home town) and working for a while as a liaison officer in charge of loading transports, Reagan was briefly assigned to the Army Air Corps. After that he spent the rest of his military career at Culver City's Hal Roach Studios, then under Army command. What type of films did the Hal Roach Studios produce during the war?

11. In 1943 the U.S. Army released Reagan for several weeks to work in an American-morale-boosting film for Warner Bros. What is the name of this film?

12. While making the film, Reagan was kept on his first lieutenant's wages. What was he making a month as a first-louie?

13. In the film, Reagan played the soldier son of a showman who had served in the First World War. What future U.S. Senator played Reagan's father?

14. What was the rank of the character Reagan portrayed?

15. The film raised millions of dollars for what type of charity?

In addition to Reagan's on-base Army duties as a narrator and director of training and professional films, he played in several of the films. Listed below on the left are three that he made at the Hal Roach Studios. Listed on the right are the characters he portrayed in those films. Match them correctly.

16. Mr. Gardenia Jones   A. Downed pilot

17. Rear Gunner   B. Catholic priest

18. For God and Country   C. Lonely soldier in a strange
                               town

19. What was Ronald Reagan's rank when he was discharged from the Army on December 9, 1945?

20. Reagan made more films before than after his three years in the regular Army. Never again would he work in anything that had the quality of Kings Row. The films that he made after his discharge were equal in number to the age of his younger son when he married in November of 1980. How many films did Ronald Reagan make after his Army discharge?

(Lt.) Ronald Reagan and Joan Leslie in Irving Berlin's *This is The Army*, a 1943 Warner Bros. film.

MORE COLOR THAN ANY OTHER MOVIE MAGAZINE

Modern Screen

OCTOBER

15¢

DELL

CAPT. RONALD REAGAN

Magazine cover showing (Captain) Ronald Reagan in a U.S. Army uniform.

RONALD REAGAN'S SCREEN NAMES QUIZ I

Listed below on the left are screen names of Ronald Reagan and on the right are the films in which these names appeared. Match the name with the film.

(Score five points for each correct answer.)

1. George Gipp
2. George Armstrong Custer
3. Drake McHugh
4. Grover Cleveland Alexander
5. Matt Sawyer
6. Jimmy Grant
7. Peter Rowan
8. Lt. Brass Bancroft
9. Eddie King
10. Pvt. Dennis Murphy
11. Jack Withering
12. Commander Casey Abbott
13. Pvt. Johnny Jones
14. Professor John Palmer
15. Professor Peter Boyd
16. Jack Miller
17. John Lawrence
18. Tom Bates
19. Steve Talbot
20. Dan McCloud

A. Flight Patrol
B. Tugboat Annie Sails Again
C. Hellcats of the Navy
D. She's Working Her Way Through College
E. Juke Girl
F. Knute Rockne- All American
G. Nine Lives Are Not Enough
H. Sergeant Murphy
I. Tropic Zone
J. Santa Fe Trail
K. Million Dollar Baby
L. Going Places
M. Bedtime for Bonzo
N. That Hagen Girl
O. The Winning Team
P. This Is the Army
Q. Kings Row
R. John Loves Mary
S. Secret Service of the Air
T. Swing Your Lady

Ronald Reagan clutches the hand of Ann Sheridan in this scene from the
Warner-National film *Juke Girl*, (1942).

Walter Slezak watches Ronald Reagan
bottle-feed the chimp, Bonzo, in this scene from
It's Showtime, released by United Artists.

Scene from *Desperate Journey*, starring Ronald Reagan and Alan Hale.

RONALD REAGAN'S SCREEN NAMES QUIZ II

Listed below on the left are screen names of Ronald Reagan and on the right are the films in which these names appeared. Match the name with the film.

(Score five points for each correct answer.)

1.	Web Sloane	A.	Stallion Road
2.	Jeff Williams	B.	Law and Order
3.	Alex Hamm	C.	Louisa
4.	Mr. Browning	D.	Girls on Probation
5.	Larry Hanraham	E.	Code of the Secret Service
6.	Yank	F.	Prisoner of War
7.	Pat Remsen	G.	The Hasty Heart
8.	Johnny Hammond	H.	Storm Warning
9.	Frame Johnson	I.	The Bad Man
10.	Bill Page	J.	Brother Rat
11.	Burt Rainey	K.	Hong Kong
12.	Vance Britten	L.	Angels Wash Their Faces
13.	Hal Norton	M.	The Voice of the Turtle
14.	Pat Dunn	N.	The Last Outpost
15.	Gil Jones	O.	Accidents Will Happen
16.	Ed Clark	P.	Dark Victory
17.	Eric Gregg	Q.	Cowboy from Brooklyn
18.	Neil Dillon	R.	Naughty but Nice
19.	Dan Crawford	S.	Desperate Journey
20.	Lt. Brass Bancroft	T.	The Killers

Ronald Reagan about to be hanged in this scene from the 1941 MGM release,
The Bad Man.

In the 1951 Warner Bros. film, *Storm Warning,*
Ronald Reagan portrayed an enemy of the
Ku Klux Klan.

RONALD REAGAN'S SCREEN PROFESSIONS QUIZ I

Listed below on the left are the names of 20 Ronald Reagan films and on the right are his screen professions. Match up the profession with the film.

(Score five points for each correct answer.)

1. The Girl from Jones Beach
2. Bedtime for Bonzo
3. Hong Kong
4. Tropic Zone
5. Juke Girl
6. The Last Outpost
7. The Winning Team
8. Knute Rockne–All American
9. Brother Rat
10. Love Is on the Air
11. Cowboy from Brooklyn
12. Sergeant Murphy
13. Stallion Road
14. Smashing the Money Ring
15. The Voice of the Turtle
16. Night unto Night
17. Cattle Queen of Montana
18. Santa Fe Trail
19. Hellcats of the Navy
20. International Squadron

A. Veterinarian
B. Flyer
C. Soldier
D. Cowpoke
E. Baseball player
F. Football player
G. Artist
H. Banana plantation foreman
I. Adventurer/soldier of fortune
J. College professor
K. Farm laborer
L. Confederate cavalry officer
M. Union cavalry officer
N. Naval commander
O. Scientist
P. V.M.I. cadet
Q. Cavalry private
R. Radio announcer
S. Press agent
T. Secret Serviceman

Warner Bros. ad for *The Girl From Jones Beach*.

RONALD REAGAN'S SCREEN PROFESSIONS QUIZ II

Listed below on the left are the names of 20 Ronald Reagan films and on the right are his screen professions. Match up the profession with the film.

(Score five points for each correct answer.)

1. She's Working Her Way Through College
2. This Is the Army
3. Murder in the Sky
4. Boy Meets Girl
5. Girls on Probation
6. Storm Warning
7. Angels Wash Their Faces
8. Hell's Kitchen
9. Naughty but Nice
10. An Angel from Texas
11. Tugboat Annie Sails Again
12. Nine Lives Are Not Enough
13. Law and Order
14. Desperate Journey
15. Desperate Journey
15. International Squadron
16. The Bad Man
17. Million Dollar Baby
18. Kings Row
19. Dark Victory
20. Swing Your Lady

A. D.A.'s son
B. Sailor
C. Flight officer
D. Sports reporter
E. Piano player
F. College professor
G. Playboy
H. Soldier
I. Radio announcer
J. Railroad worker
K. Secret Serviceman
L. Cowboy
M. Lawyer
N. Social worker
O. District attorney
P. Broadway producer
Q. Crime reporter
R. R.A.F. flyer
S. Sheriff
T. Music publisher

THIS IS A STORY WITH A LOT OF *Twists!*

WOW! LOOK HOW

"She's Working Her Way Through College"

COLOR BY **TECHNICOLOR**

She's a burlesque cutie who zips out of the runway and into college—then puts some brand new shakes in Shakespeare!

GAY GARTERS GERTIE!

WE WANT GERTIE!

VIRGINIA'S GOT GENE NELSON DANCING ON THE WALLS!

THE CHEERLEADER OF MUSICAL ENTERTAINMENTS FROM WARNER BROS!

STARRING VIRGINIA **MAYO** · RONALD **REAGAN** · GENE **NELSON**

ON DeFORE   PHYLLIS THAXTER   PATRICE WYMORE   DIRECTED BY BRUCE HUMBERSTONE   SCREEN PLAY BY PETER MILNE   PRODUCED BY WILLIAM JACOBS

Musical Numbers Staged & Directed by LeRoy Prinz · Musical Direction Ray Heindorf

Ronald Reagan was a featured performer in the Warner Bros. musical, *She's Working Her Way Through College.*

21

RONALD REAGAN'S LEADING LADIES QUIZ I

Listed below on the left are the leading ladies of 20 Ronald Reagan films and on the right are the films. Match the leading lady with the film.

(Score five points for each correct answer.)

1.	June Travis	A.	Tugboat Annie Sails Again
2.	Mary Maguire	B.	International Squadron
3.	Jane Bryan	C.	This Is the Army
4.	Margaret Lindsay	D.	Storm Warning
5.	Ann Sheridan	E.	Night unto Night
6.	Margot Stevenson	F.	Love Is on the Air
7.	Rosella Towne	G.	Sergeant Murphy
8.	Lya Lys	H.	Murder in the Sky
9.	Jane Wyman	I.	Million Dollar Baby
10.	Priscilla Lane	J.	Girls on Probation
11.	Joan Perry	K.	Hell's Kitchen
12.	Olympe Bradne	L.	Code of the Secret Service
13.	Joan Leslie	M.	The Voice of the Turtle
14.	Ronda Fleming	N.	John Loves Mary
15.	Shirley Temple	O.	Smashing the Money Ring
16.	Eleanor Parker	P.	Angels Wash Their Faces
17.	Patricia Neal	Q.	Nine Lives Are Not Enough
18.	Vivica Lindfors	R.	That Hagen Girl
19.	Virginia Mayo	S.	Hong Kong
20.	Ginger Rogers	T.	The Girl from Jones Beach

Ronald Reagan escorting Ruth Roman at a
Hollywood affair during his bachelor days.

Ronald Reagan and Ann Sheridan in this scene
from the 1942 Warner Bros. film, *Kings Row*.

RONALD REAGAN'S LEADING LADIES QUIZ II

Listed below on the left are 20 Ronald Reagan leading ladies and on the right are the films. Match the leading lady with the film.

(Score five points for each correct answer.)

1.	Ann Sheridan	A.	Boy Meets Girl
2.	Patricia Neal	B.	Stallion Road
3.	Rhonda Fleming	C.	Going Places
4.	Ruth Hussey	D.	The Bad Man
5.	Diana Lynn	E.	Kings Row
6.	Phyllis Thaxter	F.	Louisa
7.	Doris Day	G.	The Hasty Heart
8.	Dorothy Malone	H.	An Angel from Texas
9.	Barbara Stanwyck	I.	The Last Outpost
10.	Nancy Davis	J.	Hollywood Hotel
11.	Angie Dickinson	K.	Dark Victory
12.	Gloria Blondell	L.	Cowboy from Brooklyn
13.	Laraine Day	M.	Law and Order
14.	Alexis Smith	N.	She's Working Her Way Through College
15.	Jane Wyman		
16.	Bette Davis	O.	Bedtime for Bonzo
17.	Priscilla Lane	P.	The Winning Team
18.	Rosemary Lane	Q.	Accidents Will Happen
19.	Marie Wilson	R.	Hellcats of the Navy
20.	Anita Louise	S.	The Killers
		T.	Cattle Queen of Montana

the FUNNIEST thing that ever happened to a family!

POP lost his vice-presidency!

MOM lost her peace of mind!

The GROCER lost his heart!

The TYCOON lost his shirt!

SISTER lost her boy friend!

GRANDMA lost her manners!

SONNY lost his appetite!

The BOY FRIEND lost his voice!

The MAID lost her patience!

all because of

Louisa
A UNIVERSAL-INTERNATIONAL PICTURE

"THE WHOLE FAMILY'S NUTS!"

From the Company that gave you such comedy hits as "THE EGG AND I," "FAMILY HONEYMOON," and "FRANCIS."

Starring

Ronald **REAGAN** · Charles **COBURN** · Ruth **HUSSEY** · Edmund **GWENN** · Spring **BYINGTON**

with Piper **LAURIE** · Scotty **BECKETT**   Story and Screenplay by STANLEY ROBERTS · Directed by ALEXANDER HALL · Produced by ROBERT ARTHUR

Universal-International movie ad for *Louisa* (1950), in which Ronald Reagan has trouble with his mother, played by Spring Byington and her two elderly beaus, Charles Coburn and Edmund Gwenn.

25

RONALD REAGAN MOVIE GENRE QUIZ I

Listed below on the left are the titles of 20 Ronald Reagan films and on the right are the genre of said films. Match the films with the correct category.

(Score five points for each correct answer.)

1. Cowboy from Brooklyn
2. Dark Victory
3. Angels Wash Their Faces
4. Tugboat Annie Sails Again
5. Knute Rockne–All American
6. Accidents Will Happen
7. Boy Meets Girl
8. Santa Fe Trail
9. The Bad Man
10. Brother Rat
11. Secret Service of the Air
12. Love Is on the Air
13. Sergeant Murphy
14. Naughty but Nice
15. An Angel from Texas
16. Swing Your Lady
17. Girls on Probation
18. Hollywood Hotel
19. Going Places
20. Hell's Kitchen

A. Western drama
B. Insurance drama
C. Cavalry drama
D. Social worker's drama
E. T-men melodrama
F. College comedy
G. Rodeo musical
H. Radio drama
I. Hollywood musical
J. Abolitionist drama
K. Dockside comedy
L. Football drama
M. Broadway comedy
N. Arsonist drama
O. Hillbilly comedy
P. Melodrama
Q. Hollywood comedy
R. Horse-racing musical comedy
S. Tragic melodrama
T. Musical comedy

RONALD REAGAN MOVIE GENRE QUIZ II

Listed below on the left are the titles of 20 Ronald Reagan films and on the right are the genre of said films. Match the films with the correct category.

(Score five points for each correct answer.)

1. Cattle Queen of Montana	A.	WW II adventure/drama
2. International Squadron	B.	New York sophisticated comedy
3. Nine Lives Are Not Enough	C.	Romantic comedy
4. Kings Row	D.	Army musical
5. Juke Girl	E.	Montana Western
6. Desperate Journey	F.	Central American drama
7. This Is the Army	G.	Oriental drama
8. Stallion Road	H.	KKK drama
9. Prisoner of War	I.	Melodrama
10. The Voice of the Turtle	J.	Horse-breeding drama
11. Night unto Night	K.	R.A.F. drama
12. Hellcats of the Navy	L.	Migratory workers drama
13. It's a Great Feeling	M.	Newspaper drama
14. The Hasty Heart	N.	Small-town melodrama
15. Louisa	O.	Hollywood musical comedy
16. Storm Warning	P.	Navy drama
17. The Last Outpost	Q.	WW II melodrama
18. Hong Kong	R.	Civil War Western
19. The Winning Team	S.	Baseball drama
20. Tropic Zone	T.	Korean drama

RONALD REAGAN FILM GEOGRAPHY QUIZ

The 20 questions listed below deal with the geographical locations (real or fictitious) of Ronald Reagan films.

(Score five points for each correct answer.)

1. Name the film with a borough of New York in the title.

2. Name the film with an Asian seaport in the title.

3. Name the film with a fictitious midwestern town at the turn-of-the-century in the title.

4. Name the film with the 16th state (admitted to the Union) in the title (capital: Nashville).

5. Name the film with the 40th state (admitted to the Union) in the title (capital: Helena).

6. Name the film which had a fictitious street of horse-breeders in the title.

7. In what country did Prisoner of War take place?

8. In what country did International Squadron take place?

9. In what state did Juke Girl take place?

10. In what country did Desperate Journey take place?

11. Name the film in which a popular American resort area appears.

12. Name the film with a California city in the title.

13. Name the film with the 39th state (admitted to the Union) in the title (capital: Austin.)

14. Name the film with the capital of New Mexico in the title.

15. In what city and state does Law and Order take place?

16. In what fictitious South American country does Tropic Zone take place?

17. For what city's team did Ronald Reagan play baseball in The Winning Team?

18. In what state does <u>The Last Outpost</u> take place?

19. In what country does <u>The Hasty Heart</u> take place?

20. In what state does <u>Night unto Night</u> take place?

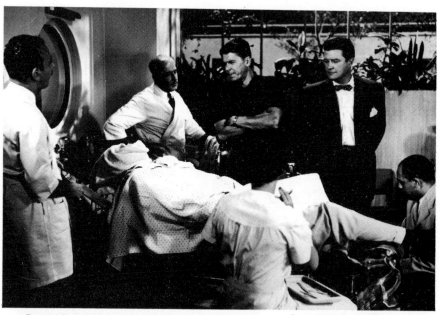

Ronald Reagan, who was not included in the cast of the film, appeared briefly in a scene as "guest star" in *It's A Great Feeling*. This 1949 Warner Bros. release starred Dennis Morgan (right).

Ronald Reagan being made up with a patent-leather hairdo and moustache for a screen test.

RONALD REAGAN'S SCREEN DIRECTORS QUIZ I

Listed below on the left are 20 Ronald Reagan films and on the right are the 20 directors. Match the film with the correct director.

(Score five points for each correct answer.)

1.	Bedtime for Bonzo	A.	Lloyd Bacon
2.	John Loves Mary	B.	Frederick de Cordova
3.	Dark Victory	C.	Don Siegel
4.	Santa Fe Trail	D.	Stuart Heisler
5.	Million Dollar Baby	E.	Allan Dwan
6.	Kings Row	F.	Andrew Marton
7.	International Squadron	G.	Edward Sutherland
8.	Desperate Journey	H.	Edmund Goulding
9.	Stallion Road	I.	Michael Curtiz
10.	The Voice of the Turtle	J.	Sam Wood
11.	Night unto Night	K.	Curtis Bernhardt
12.	The Hasty Heart	L.	Vincent Sherman
13.	Storm Warning	M.	Bruce Humberstone
14.	She's Working Her Way Through College	N.	Lewis R. Foster
15.	That Hagen Girl	O.	David Butler
16.	Nine Lives Are Not Enough	P.	Lewis Seiler
17.	Cattle Queen of Montana	Q.	Irving Rapper
18.	Tropic Zone	R.	Raoul Walsh
19.	Prisoner of War	S.	James V. Kern
20.	Knute Rockne–All American	T.	Peter Godfrey

Ronald Reagan gets his boots dirtied by a wardrobe make-up specialist for an escape scene in *Desperate Journey* (1942).

RONALD REAGAN'S SCREEN DIRECTORS QUIZ II

Listed below on the left are 20 Ronald Reagan films and on the right are the directors. Match the film and the director.

(Score five points for each correct answer.)

1.	Tugboat Annie Sails Again	A.	William Keighley
2.	The Girl from Jones Beach	B.	Nathan Juran
3.	Louisa	C.	Noel Smith
4.	Juke Girl	D.	David Butler
5.	Hong Kong	E.	Lewis Seller
6.	Love Is on the Air	F.	William McGann
7.	Hollywood Hotel	G.	Alexander Hall
8.	Swing Your Lady	H.	William Clemens
9.	Cowboy from Brooklyn	I.	Peter Godfrey
10.	Brother Rat	J.	Lewis R. Foster
11.	The Bad Man	K.	B. Reeves Eason
12.	This Is the Army	L.	Ray Enright
13.	It's a Great Feeling	M.	Don Siegel
14.	Law and Order	N.	Curtis Bernhardt
15.	Tennessee's Partner	O.	Busby Berkeley
16.	The Killers	P.	Lloyd Bacon
17.	Accidents Will Happen	Q.	Richard Thorpe
18.	Sergeant Murphy	R.	Allan Dwan
19.	Girls on Probation	S.	Michael Curtiz
20.	Secret Service of the Air	T.	Bryan Foy

Ronald Reagan's brother, Neal, in his first movie, *Destroyer* (1943), pictured here with Edward G. Robinson. Like his brother Ronald, Neal started in radio.

SONGS FROM RONALD REAGAN FILMS QUIZ

Listed below on the left are 20 songs from Ronald Reagan films and on the right are the films. Match the songs with the films.

(Score five points for each correct answer.)

1. "Oh, How I Hate to Get up in the Morning"

2. "Jeepers Creepers"

3. "Ride, Tenderfoot, Ride"

4. "God Bless America"

5. "Silhouetted in Moonlight"

6. "Give Me a Song with a Beautiful Melody"

7. "I Left My Heart at the Stage Door Canteen"

8. "I'll Dream Tonight"

9. "Let That Be a Lesson to You"

10. "Oh, Give Me Time for Tenderness"

11. "Mandy"

12. "Hooray for Hollywood"

13. "At the Cafe Rendezvous"

14. "I Found a Million Dollar Baby From the 5 & 10¢ Store"

15. "Your Country and My Country"

16. "I've hitched My Wagon to a Star"

17. "I'm Getting Tired So I Can Sleep"

18. "Hooray for Spinach"

19. "Dig Me a Grave in Missouri"

20. "Can't Teach My Old Heart New Tricks"

A. Dark Victory

B. It's a Great Feeling

C. This Is the Army

D. Hollywood Hotel

E. Cowboy from Brooklyn

F. Naughty but Nice

G. Swing Your Lady

H. Going Places

I. Million Dollar Baby

Movie ad for *John Loves Mary* (1949). This film introduced Patricia Neal to the screen, after her Broadway success in Lillian Hellman's *Another Part of the Forest*.

AUTHORS OF RONALD REAGAN FILMS QUIZ

Listed below on the left are the authors of 20 Ronald Reagan films and on the right are the films. Match the authors with the films.

(Score five points for each correct answer.)

1. Bella and Sam Spewack
2. John Monks, Jr. and Fred F. Finkelhoffe
3. George E. Brewer, Jr. and Bertram Bloch
4. Norman Reilly Raine
5. Porter Emerson Brown
6. Henry Bellaman
7. Stephen Longstreet
8. Edith Roberts
9. John Van Druten
10. Norman Krasna
11. Philip Wylie
12. Allen Boretz
13. John Patrick
14. Elliott Nugent
15. Ernest Hemingway
16. Bret Harte
17. Irving Berlin
18. Louis Peletier, Jr. and Robert Sloane
19. George S. Kaufman
20. Victor Mapes and William Collier, Sr.

A. John Loves Mary
B. This Is the Army
C. Going Places (The Hottentot)
D. The Hasty Heart
E. Boy Meets Girl
F. An Angel from Texas (The Bread and Butter Man)
G. Brother Rat
H. John Loves Mary
I. Tugboat Annie Sails Again
J. She's Working Her Way Through College (The Male Animal)
K. Cowboy from Brooklyn (Howdy Stranger)
L. Kings Row
M. Dark Victory
N. Stallion Road
O. Night unto Night
P. The Bad Man
Q. That Hagen Girl
R. The Girl from Jones Beach
S. The Voice of the Turtle
T. Tennessee's Partner

Movie ad for *Tugboat Annie Sails Again* (1940), which starred Marjorie Rambeau (in the title role) and Alan Hale. Ronald Reagan and Jane Wyman were billed as those "loveable sweethearts."

RONALD REAGAN SCRAMBLED MOVIE TITLES QUIZ

Listed below are the scrambled titles of 20 Ronald Reagan films. Identify these films.

(Score five points for each correct answer.)

1. NGSIK OWR
2. NOHG GNOK
3. PRITOC ENOZ
4. TEH TYSHA RAHTE
5. HTE STAL POOTTSU
6. TSEGNEAR HPYURM
7. ETH LELIRSK
8. AISOLU
9. HORRBET TRA
10. LOSTANLI ODAR
11. KUJE LIRG
12. NAATS EF LIRAT
13. ROSMT NANWRIG
14. TEH GNNNIIW AMET
15. NOJH OSLEV ARMY
16. WLA NAD DEORR
17. RADK CROITVY
18. GGNIO CLEPAS
19. ETH ABD NMA
20. WYOHLOYDL TOLEH

RONALD REAGAN'S MOVIE TITLES DAFFY-NITIONS QUIZ

Listed below are the "daffy-nitions" of 20 titles of Ronald Reagan's films. Identify the films.

(Score five points for each correct answer.)

1. Priceless infant
2. An inn for the stars
3. Amour on the radio
4. Hillbilly state's cohort
5. Asian port
6. They didn't lose
7. Heavenly cherubs clean up
8. Sibling rodent
9. Sibling rodent and offspring
10. Nighty-night for chimp
11. The awful guy
12. Hurricane alarm
13. Horse street
14. Record-box lass
15. Critical trip
16. Miss Alcott
17. Equatorial climate area
18. The liquidators
19. Westerner from New York borough
20. Dim wit

KING'S ROW QUIZ I

Every critic agrees that <u>Kings Row</u> was one of Ronald Reagan's best films. Listed below are 20 questions concerning that film.

(Score five points for each correct answer.)

1. Who directed <u>Kings Row</u>?
2. Who wrote the novel on which the film was based?
3. Who wrote the screenplay?
4. Who was the well-known cinematographer?
5. Who composed the background music?
6. Who did the art and set direction?
7. What was Ronald Reagan's name in the film?
8. What was Ann Sheridan's name in the film?
9. What was Robert Cummings' name in the film?
10. What was Betty Field's name in the film?
11. Who played the two men as boys?
12. Who played the two women as girls?
13. Who portrayed Dr. Henry Gordon in the film?
14. Who portrayed Mrs. Henry Gordon in the film?
15. Who portrayed Dr. Alexander Tower in the film?
16. Who portrayed Louise Gordon in the film?
17. Who portrayed Elise Sandor in the film?
18. Who portrayed Madame Von Eln in the film?
19. Who portrayed Colonel Skeffington in the film?
20. Who portrayed Pa Monahan in the film?

Two scenes from *Kings Row* (1942). Photo above is a rehearsal for the famous "bed scene." Photo below shows Ann and Ronnie in the "Where's the rest of me?" scene.

KINGS ROW QUIZ II

The 20 questions below deal with Casey Robinson's screen treatment rather than the Henry Bellaman novel.

(Score five points for each correct answer.)

1. Why did Dr. Towers kill Cassandra, then commit suicide?
2. How did Drake lose his family inheritance?
3. What were the names of the two high-spirited sisters with whom Drake "fooled around"?
4. To whom did Drake apply for a job?
5. What was this man's position?
6. What caused Drake's accident?
7. Who decided to amputate both legs?
8. Why did he make this decision?
9. Who revealed to Parris the truth about the amputation?
10. Who confirmed this, having held the lantern for the doctor?
11. Of what does Parris' grandmother die?
12. Where does Parris go to study medicine?
13. Who was originally slated to play Dr. Tower?
14. Why did he not?
15. Whom did Warner Bros. want to cast as Parris?
16. What two top Warner Bros. actresses wanted to play Cassandra?
17. What four other Warner Bros. actors were considered for the part of Drake?
18. What was the famous line spoken by Drake when he discovers the amputation?
19. What were Randy's lines when she leaves Drake's room immediately after?
20. What prompts Parris to fall in love with Elise Sandor?

A portrait of film star Ronald Reagan taken by
Warner Bros. photographer Madison Lacy when
Ron starred in the Warner Bros. production of
King's Row.

SANTA FE TRAIL QUIZ

Santa Fe Trail gave Ronald Reagan one of the three real-life roles in his career. Listed below are 20 questions concerning this film.

(Score five points for each correct answer.)

1. Who directed Santa Fe Trail?

2. Who was the cinematographer?

3. Who composed the background music?

4. What real-life role did Ronald Reagan play?

5. What real-life role did Errol Flynn play?

6. Who played abolitionist John Brown?

7. Who played two of John Brown's sons in the film?

8. Who played Robert E. Lee?

9. Who played Phil Sheridan?

10. Who played Jefferson Davis?

11. Who played George Pickett?

12. Who played James Longstreet?

13. Who played John Bell Hood?

14. Who played the role of Charlotte, the girl Ronald Reagan ends up with, having lost Olivia de Havilland to Errol Flynn?

15. This actress was nominated in 1942 for a Best Supporting Actress award in what film?

16. In this film, where are Custer and Stuart stationed?

17. The actors all played cadets at what school?

18. What town did John Brown take over?

19. Who was the colonel who subdued John Brown?

20. What was the name of the film in which Errol Flynn played Custer?

It's Here!
The thundering story that
challenges all filmdom to
match its excitement!
"Iron Rails to Kansas . . .
Iron Nerves from there on!"

WARNER BROS. PRESENT ERROL FLYNN
OLIVIA DE HAVILLAND
in
Santa Fe Trail
A thousand miles of danger with a thousand thrills a mile!

Original Screen Play
by Robert Buckner
Music by Max Steiner

WATCH!
The big hit right after
'Santa Fe Trail' will be
'FOUR MOTHERS'
It's the wonderful new
Warner Bros. picture
starring the 'Four
Daughters'!

Movie ad for *Santa Fe Trail* (1940), starring Errol Flynn and Olivia de Havilland, with Ronald Reagan portraying a young George Armstrong Custer. Reagan received fourth billing.

STORM WARNING QUIZ

(Score five points for each correct answer.)

1. Who directed Storm Warning?
2. What studio produced it?
3. Who was the producer?
4. Who wrote the original story?
5. Who was the costume designer?
6. Ginger Rogers and Doris Day were sisters in the film. Which one was married?
7. To whom was she married?
8. What was his occupation?
9. What was Ronald Reagan's occupation?
10. What was Ginger Rogers' occupation?
11. To what organization does Steve Cochran belong?
12. What event does Ginger Rogers inadvertently witness?
13. What actress was originally slated for the Ginger Rogers role?
14. Why did she back out of the part?
15. Much of the film was shot on location in a small California town. What was this town?
16. In 1937 Warner Bros. made another film indicting the KKK. What was the film?
17. Who was the male star?
18. Who was the female star?
19. Who played the two secondary leads?
20. Who directed this film?

Movie ad for *Storm Warning* (1951), in which Ronald Reagan portrayed a district attorney in a small Southern town who successfully indicts the Ku Klux Klan.

BROTHER RAT QUIZ

Brother Rat and its sequel, Brother Rat and a Baby, are important in Ronald Reagan's career because both teamed him with Jane Wyman, the first Mrs. Ronald Reagan. Listed below are 20 questions concerning these two films.

(Score five points for each correct answer.)

1. Who wrote the original play on which these films were based?

2. Who played the male lead of Billy Randolph?

3. Who played the male lead of Bing Edwards?

4. Who played the male lead of Dan Crawford?

5. At what school are these three cadets?

6. Who played the female lead of Joyce Winfree?

7. Who played the female lead of Claire Adams?

8. Who played the female lead of Kate Rice?

9. What sport did the three cadets play?

10. What is Bing's burden in the first film?

11. What complicates Dan and Claire's romance?

12. Of the three male leads, only Eddie Albert was nominated for an Oscar (for Best Supporting Actor) twice. What were the films?

13. What actress did Eddie Albert marry?

14. What is the name of their well-known actor son?

15. In Brother Rat and a Baby, who plays Jane Wyman's father, the VMI commandant?

16. What is the name Bing and Kate call their baby?

17. What job are Billy and Dan trying to secure for Bing?

18. Where does Billy plant the baby to gain publicity for Bing?

19. One of the six leads died in 1959. Who was it?

20. One of the six leads retired from acting in 1941. Who was it?

Two scenes from *Brother Rat* (1938) which
co-starred Wayne Morris, Johnnie Davis,
Eddie Albert and Ronald Reagan.

KNUTE ROCKNE–ALL AMERICAN QUIZ

This film was credited with lifting Ronald Reagan from the B's and starting him on his way to top stardom. Listed below are 20 questions concerning the film.

(Score five points for each correct answer.)

1. Who directed Knute Rockne–All American?

2. Who was the cinematographer?

3. Who composed the background music?

4. Who played Knute Rockne?

5. What role did Ronald Reagan play?

6. What was Ronald Reagan's nickname in the film?

7. What did Pat O'Brien do in this film that revealed his devout Catholicism?

8. At what Catholic college did the film take place?

9. Who played Mrs. Knute Rockne?

10. Of what did Ronald Reagan's character die?

11. After his death, what were his teammates exhorted to do?

12. What position did Ronald Reagan play in this film?

13. Who played Knute Rockne's father and mother?

14. Who played Knute Rockne as a boy?

15. For what other role was this child actor noted?

16. What were Ronald Reagan and three of his teammates nicknamed?

17. In what country was Knute Rockne born?

18. From what affliction did Knute Rockne suffer?

19. How did Knute Rockne die?

20. What were Ronald Reagan's lines to Pat O'Brien on his deathbed?

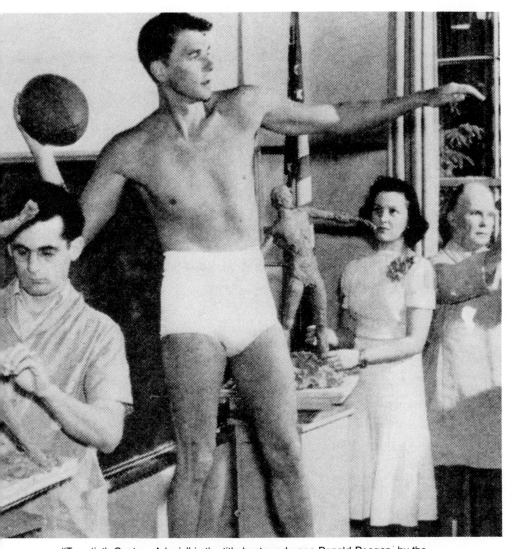

"Twentieth Century Adonis" is the title bestowed upon Ronald Reagan, by the Division of Fine Arts of the University of Southern California. Reagan, a Warner Bros. actor, is shown posing for Professor Merrel's (in smock) sculpturing class, and was said to possess the most nearly perfect male figure.

RONALD REAGAN'S HOLLYWOOD FRIENDS QUIZ

Listed below are descriptions of some of Ronald Reagan's friends.

(Score five points for each correct answer.)

1. Attending Jane Wyman's farewell party before Ronald Reagan left for the Army in 1942 was: a frequent co-star, a beautiful redhead from Texas.

2. Ditto above: her actor-husband of the time, from Dublin.

3. Ditto above: a well-known comedian from Waukegan, Illinois.

4. Ditto above: his equally well-known wife.

5. Ditto above: a well-known actress whose real name was Ruby Stevens.

6. Ditto above: a well-known actor whose real name was Spangler Brugh.

7. Ditto above: a well-known actor and wife, Mr. "Knute Rockne."

8. What Hollywood couple "stood up" for Ronald Reagan and Nancy Davis at their wedding?

9. Lanky actor who portrayed Mr. Smith and Monty Stratton.

10. Old blue eyes.

11. Dino.

12. The master of insults.

13. Handsome Australian actor, frequent co-star.

14. Sister of Joan Fontaine.

15. Member of famous Hollywood and Broadway acting family.

16. Tenor of many Warner Bros. musicals.

17. Leading man, former husband of Anne Shirley and Gloria de Haven.

18. Lovely blonde, leading lady in <u>Going Places</u>.

19. Lovely blonde, leading lady in <u>Sing Me a Love Song</u>.

20. Former crooner who turned to tough-guy roles.

Relaxing from his duties as President of the
Screen Actors Guild, Ronald Reagan dines with
Ruth Roman at Ciro's in Hollywood in 1950.

Keeping in shape, Ronald Reagan plays ball with orchestra leader Johnny Davis and
actor John Payne in the early 1940s.

RONALD REAGAN'S FRIENDS AND FILM CO-WORKERS QUIZ

Listed below on the left are the original names of 20 people Ronald Reagan has known personally and/or has appeared with in films. To confuse you further, the original names of those he appeared with in films are marked with an asterisk. The pseudonyms are on the right. Match them to the names on the left.

(Score five points for each correct answer.)

1.	Betty Perske	A.	Dean Martin
2.	Marilyn Louis*	B.	June Allyson
3.	Doris Van Kappelhof*	C.	William Holden
4.	Francis Timothy Durgin*	D.	Rory Calhoun
5.	Frances Gumm	E.	Doris Day
6.	Archibald Leach	F.	Joe Louis
7.	Edith Marrener*	G.	Rhonda Fleming
8.	William Beedle	H.	Ginger Rogers
9.	Rosetta Jacobs*	I.	Edward G. Robinson
10.	Herman Brix*	J.	Eve Arden
11.	Eunice Quedens*	K.	Danny Thomas
12.	Benjamin Kubelsky	L.	John Wayne
13.	Amos Jacobs	M.	Judy Garland
14.	Marion Morrison	N.	Susan Hayward
15.	Emanuel Goldenberg	O.	Bruce Bennett
16.	Leonard Slye	P.	Lauren Bacall
17.	Joe L. Barrow*	Q.	Jack Benny
18.	Virginia McMath*	R.	Piper Laurie
19.	Dino Crocetti	S.	Gary Grant
20.	Ella Geisman	T.	Roy Rogers

Ronald Reagan and his date, Florence Murray,
enjoy the opening night performance at the
Players Ring in Hollywood.

Ronald Reagan and wife, Jane Wyman, about to
order dinner in a Hollywood restaurant.

RONALD REAGAN FILM ANTONYMS QUIZ

How many of the 20 Ronald Reagan films from which the antonyms below have been derived can you identify?

(Score five points for each correct answer.)

1. "The Silent Reptile"

2. "Balmy Forecast"

3. "Day into Day"

4. "It's a Putrid Perception"

5. "Bright Defeat"

6. "The Good Woman"

7. "Bankrupt Octogenarian"

8. "One Death Is More Than Sufficient"

9. "Mare Street"

10. "The First Fort"

11. "The Slow Organ"

12. "The Losing Congregation"

13. "The Pacifists"

14. "Hate Is in the Earth"

15. "Polar Region"

16. "Crime and Chaos"

17. "Heaven's Hallway"

18. "Devils Dirty Their Countenances"

19. "Good but Nasty"

20. "Staying Still"

Movie ad for *The Voice of the Turtle* (1947), which co-starred Eleanor Parker. This was Ronald Reagan's third postwar film that also featured Eve Arden and Wayne Morris in supporting roles.

OSCAR WINNERS AND NOMINEES IN
RONALD REAGAN FILMS QUIZ I

Listed below are films in which Ronald Reagan appeared with winners and nominees of Oscars. Identify the winners or nominees (as indicated) and the films involved.

(Score five points for each correct answer.)

1. Dark Victory (Winner, Best Actress, two films)
2. Kings Row (Nominee, Supporting Actress, two films)
3. Louisa (Winner, Supporting Actor, one film)
4. Louisa (Winner, Supporting Actor, one film)
5. Santa Fe Trail (Winner, Best Actress, two films)
6. Knute Rockne-All American (Winner, Supporting Actor, one film)
7. Night unto Night (Winner, Best Actor, one film)
8. International Squadron (Nominee, Supporting Actor, one film)
9. Boy Meets Girl (Nominee, Supporting Actor, one film)
10. The Hasty Heart (Winner, Best Actress, one film)
11. Dark Victory (Nominee, Supporting Actor, two films)
12. Juke Girl (Nominee, Supporting Actor, one film)
13. Girls on Probation (Winner, Best Actress, one film)
14. Desperate Journey (Nominee, Supporting Actor, one film)
15. Voice of the Turtle (Nominee, Supporting Actress, two films)
16. Santa Fe Trail (Nominee, Best Actor, one film)
17. The Bad Man (Winner, Best Actor, one film)
18. The Bad Man (Winner, Best Actor, one film)
19. Louisa (Nominee, Supporting Actress, one film)
20. Louisa (Nominee, Supporting Actress, one film)

Warner Bros. hypeing Bette Davis in *Dark Victory*.

OSCAR WINNERS AND NOMINEES IN
RONALD REAGAN FILMS QUIZ II

Listed below are films in which Ronald Reagan appeared with winners and nominees of Oscars. Identify the winners or nominees (as indicated) and the films involved.

(Score five points for each correct answer.)

1. Kings Row (Nominee, Supporting Actor, four films)
2. Prisoner of War (Nominee, Supporting Actor, one film)
3. Tugboat Annie Sails Again (Winner, Best Actress, one film)
4. Tugboat Annie Sails Again (Nominee, Supporting Actress, two films)
5. Cattle Queen of Montana (Nominee, Best Actress, four films)
6. Storm Warning (Winner, Best Actress, one film)
7. The Winning Team (Nominee, Best Actress, one film)
8. Santa Fe Trail (Winner, Supporting Actor, one film)
9. Santa Fe Trail (Nominee, Supporting Actress, one film)
10. Dark Victory (Winner, Best Actor, one film)
11. Law and Order (Winner, Supporting Actress, one film)
12. Kings Row (Nominee, Supporting Actress, one film)
13. Angels Wash Their Faces (Nominee, Supporting Actress, one film)
14. Desperate Journey (Nominee, Supporting Actor, four films)
15. The Hasty Heart (Nominee, Best Actor, one film)
16. This Is the Army (Nominee Supporting Actress, one film)
17. The Voice of the Turtle (Nominee, Best Actress, three films)
18. The Bad Man (Nominee, Supporting Actor, one film)
19. An Angel from Texas (Nominee, Supporting Actor, two films)
20. Nine Lives Are Not Enough (Nominee, Supporting Actor, one film)

Ronald Reagan and Ann Sheridan in a scene from Warner's *Kings Row*.

NANCY DAVIS MOVIE QUIZ

(Score five points for each correct answer.)

1. Name the film in which Nancy Davis and Ronald Reagan appeared together.
2. What was her occupation in this film?
3. What was his occupation in this film?
4. What war was the background for this film?
5. Her screen debut was in 1949's <u>Shadows on the Wall</u>. Who were the co-stars?
6. Her biggest success was as the lead in a 1950 quasi-religious film. Name it.
7. What part did she play in this film?
8. Who played her son?
9. Who was her co-star?
10. In 1952 they co-starred in another film. Name it.
11. Who was the third co-star?
12. In 1952 she was part of an all-star MGM cast in a film glorifying the United States. Name it.
13. In 1949 she was part of the cast in a film which co-starred Glenn Ford and Janet Leigh. Name it.
14. She played a New York socialite in a 1949 film which starred Barbara Stanwyck, James Mason and Ava Gardner. Name it.
15. A well-known female dancer also had a small supporting role in this film. Who was she?
16. In 1951 she made a film about a professor who loses his family in a fire and turns to alcohol. Name it.
17. Who were the two male stars?
18. One of these stars won an Oscar playing Don Birnham, another alcoholic. Who was he?
19. In 1952 she co-starred in <u>Talk About a Stranger</u> with an actor who also entered politics. Who was he?
20. In 1953 she appeared in a well-known science-fiction film. What was the film and who were the two male stars?

Ronald Reagan escorts actress Nancy Davis to the ballet in Hollywood before their marriage.

JANE WYMAN QUIZ I

(Score five points for each correct answer.)

1. What was Jane Wyman's real name?
2. What was her date of birth?
3. Where was she born?
4. Who was her famous mother?
5. What was Jane's mother's profession?
6. Where did Jane attend grammar school?
7. Where did Jane attend high school?
8. Where did Jane attend college?
9. Who was Jane's first husband?
10. When and where did they get married?
11. When were they divorced?
12. During what film did Jane meet Ronald Reagan?
13. When were they married?
14. What color wedding gown did she wear for this, her second marriage?
15. What is the name of their daughter?
16. When was she born?
17. What is the name of their son?
18. When was he adopted?
19. When were Jane and Ronald Reagan divorced?
20. Who were Jane's third and fourth husbands?

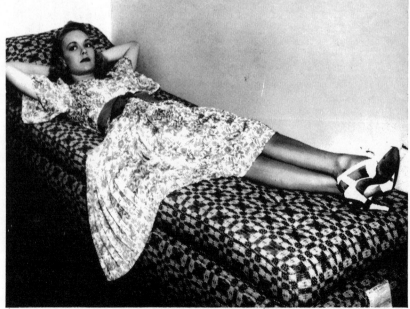

Jane Wyman featured in the Warner Bros. movie,
Brother Rat, relaxes between scenes.

Ronald Reagan and wife, Jane Wyman, frolic on a day off from the Hollywood sets.

JANE WYMAN QUIZ II

(Score five points for each correct answer.)

1. Name the four films in which Jane Wyman and Ronald Reagan appeared together.
2. Who were the other cadets in Brother Rat and its sequel besides Ronald Reagan?
3. Who were the other two females in Brother Rat and its sequel?
4. Who played the Marie Dressler/Wallace Beery roles in Tugboat Annie Sails Again?
5. What famous singer did Jane Wyman long to portray on the screen?
6. Who eventually portrayed this singer?
7. What was the film for which Jane Wyman won her Oscar?
8. What was Ronald Reagan's comment about this film at the time of their divorce?
9. For what three other films did Jane Wyman receive an Academy Award nomination?
10. What was Jane Wyman's profession in The Blue Veil?
11. What was Jane Wyman's profession in Lucy Gallant?
12. What was her profession in Three Guys Named Mike?
13. What was her physical affliction in Johnny Belinda?
14. What was her physical affliction in The Glass Menagerie?
15. What was her physical affliction in Miracle in the Rain?
16. What was her physical affliction in Magnificent Obsession?
17. Who was her leading man in My Favorite Spy?
18. Who was her leading man in Larceny, Inc.?
19. Who was her leading man in Kid Nightengale?
20. Who was her leading man in Magic Town?

Mrs. Ronald Reagan and daughter
Maureen Elizabeth Reagan.

Jane Wyman is joined by her husband Ronald
Reagan during her performance on the 1947 Lux
Radio Theater in which she did an on air-adaptation
of *Nobody Lives Forever*.

Jane Wyman, Agnes Moorehead and Lew Ayres
star in the 1948 hit, *Johnny Belinda*.

RONALD REAGAN "SUPPORTS" QUIZ I

(Score five points for each correct answer.)

1. Who was the actor appearing in International Squadron who made a memorable Hollywood debut as the Nazi pilot who invades Mrs. Miniver's kitchen?
2. Who was the actress appearing in Juke Girl who later married Elliott Roosevelt?
3. Who was the Hollywood columnist who played herself in Hollywood Hotel?
4. Who was the actress appearing in International Squadron who later married Harry Cohn, head of Columbia Studios?
5. Whose sister played Ronald Reagan's leading lady in Accidents Will Happen?
6. What actress played the scatterbrained socialite in Dark Victory?
7. What male dancer played the third lead in She's Working Her Way Through College?
8. What English actor appearing in International Squadron also appeared in the Bulldog Drummond series?
9. What character actress appearing in Kings Row was knighted (made a Dame) in England?
10. Who played the second female lead in Stallion Road?
11. Who was the actress appearing in The Voice of the Turtle who later became "Our Miss Brooks" on TV?
12. Who was the character actor appearing in Kings Row and That Hagen Girl who also played Dr. Meade in Gone With the Wind?
13. Who was the comedian appearing in John Loves Mary who got his acting training in Lela Rogers' (Ginger's mother) classes at RKO?
14. Who was the character actor appearing in Dark Victory who also appeared as the angel in James Stewart's It's a Wonderful Life?
15. Who was the comedian appearing in The Girl from Jones Beach who was the hero in Hail the Conquering Hero?
16. Who was the actress appearing in Kings Row who was Humphrey Bogart's leading lady in All Through the Night?

17. Who was the English actress appearing in <u>John Loves Mary</u> who was the long-time sweetheart of Richard Greene before he married Patricia Medina?
18. Who was the actor appearing in <u>Night unto Night</u> who won his Oscar portraying a thinly disguised Huey Long?
19. Who was the child actor appearing in <u>Louisa</u> who scored big hits in <u>Once upon a Time</u> and <u>A Tree Grows in Brooklyn</u>?
20. Who was the actress of French extract who played the lead in <u>International Squadron</u>?

Movie ad for *Stallion Road* (1947). This was Ronald Reagan's first postwar film, in which he portrayed a veterinarian who breeds horses.

RONALD REAGAN "SUPPORTS" QUIZ II

(Score five points for each correct answer.)

1. Who was the character actress appearing in Naughty but Nice who was known for her fluttery hands and her unusual voice?
2. Who was the character actor appearing in International Squadron who was nominated for his fine performance in The Letter?
3. Who was the character actor appearing in Santa Fe Trail who was almost a regular in any Errol Flynn film and who played the friend in Stella Dallas (1937)?
4. Who was the character actor appearing in Santa Fe Trail who was the other member of Errol Flynn's gang and a long-time boyfriend of Lupe Velez?
5. What young male actor appearing in Juke Girl later became a well-known Hollywood director?
6. What group of kids appeared with Ronald Reagan in The Angels Wash Their Faces and Hell's Kitchen?
7. Name the original group?
8. What title did they later take?
9. What character actor appearing in Juke Girl was nominated for Best Supporting Actor for his performance in Algiers?
10. What young actor appearing in International Squadron and Santa Fe Trail married the daughter of singer Helen Morgan?
11. What actor appearing in Desperate Journey has been nominated for Best Supporting Actor for four films?
12. Name these films.
13. What actor appearing in Nine Lives Are Not Enough was nominated for Best Supporting Actor in Here Comes Mr. Jordan?
14. Who was his actress-wife and his actor-son?
15. Who was the actress appearing in Million Dollar Baby known as "a hard-boiled blonde," who played Sam Spade's secretary in The Maltese Falcon?
16. Who was the actress appearing in She's Working Her Way Through College who was Errol Flynn's third wife?

17. Who was the character actor appearing in <u>John Loves Mary</u> who portrayed Diamond Jim Brady twice in films?
18. Name the two films.
19. He also appeared as Wall Street financier Jim Fiske in what film?
20. Who was the character actress appearing in <u>Naughty but Nice</u> whose actor-son won an Oscar in 1949?

Ronald Reagan always loved sports and playing many athletic roles. Here he is featured as George Gipp with Pat O'Brien in *Knute Rockne-All American* and as a cadet baseball player in *Brother Rat* co-starring Eddie Albert.

RONALD REAGAN "SUPPORTS" QUIZ III

(Score five points for each correct answer.)

1. Who was the character actor appearing in Hong Kong who was famous for his movie portrayal of Dr. Watson?
2. Who was the young actor appearing in Prisoner of War who played the lead in Tennessee Champ?
3. Who was the actor appearing in The Winning Team who won Joan Crawford from Robert Young in Goodbye My Fancy?
4. Who was the actor appearing in The Last Outpost and Tropic Zone whose father and uncle were also well-known actors?
5. Who was the actor appearing in Santa Fe Trail as one of John Brown's sons who specialized in playing snarling gangster roles?
6. Who was the actor appearing in Desperate Journey who was the English child-actor lead in Thoroughbreds Don't Cry?
7. Who played the Oriental boy in Hong Kong?
8. Who was the actress appearing in Dark Victory who was nominated for Best Supporting Actress in Wuthering Heights?
9. Who was the singer appearing in This Is the Army who was known in the 1930s as "The Songbird of the South"?
10. Who was the actress appearing in Night unto Night who was famous for her mother roles (mother of Sabu, Doris Day, James Cagney, et al.)?
11. Who was the actor appearing in Stallion Road who played the lead in The Mask of Demetrius?
12. Who was the character actor appearing in Bedtime for Bonzo who played the Nazi in Lifeboat and Once upon a Honeymoon?
13. Who was the English peeress, mother of a Hollywood leading man, who appeared in Hong Kong?
14. Who is the actor appearing in Prisoner of War who is the real-life brother of actor Dana Andrews?
15. Who is the actor appearing in The Last Outpost who once portrayed Tarzan in a film?
16. What was the title of this Tarzan film?

17. What was this virile athlete's real name?
18. Who was the character actor appearing in Prisoner of War who was nominated for Best Supporting Actor in I Remember Mama?
19. Who was the songwriter who appeared as a doughboy in This Is the Army?
20. Who was the character actor who appeared in several Ronald Reagan Secret Service films as his superior officer?

Ronald Reagan and Lucille Barkley in a scene from Bedtime For Bonzo.

RONALD REAGAN "SUPPORTS" QUIZ IV

(Score five points for each correct answer.)

1. Who was the actress appearing in Tennessee's Partner who also played the female lead in Tyrone Power's Nightmare Alley?
2. Who was the actor appearing in Santa Fe Trail who won his Oscar in 1941 for Johnny Eager?
3. Who was the boy-actor appearing in Santa Fe Trail who was also the star of Gallant Sons?
4. Who was the character actor appearing in Desperate Journey who was the victim in Foreign Correspondent?
5. Who was the character actress appearing in Desperate Journey who was the real-life wife of the above actor?
6. Who was the character actor appearing in This is the Army who was a witness to the movie marriage of Ronald Reagan and Joan Leslie?
7. Who was the Latin singer-dancer in Tropic Zone?
8. Who was the character actor appearing in Santa Fe Trail who portrayed Olivia de Havilland's father in Dodge City?
9. Who was the famous "torch singer" appearing in This Is the Army whose big hit of the 1930s was "Where Are You?"
10. Who was the character actor appearing in Santa Fe Trail who played the lead in the TV series "Wagon Train" for many years?
11. Who was the actor appearing in Tropic Zone who was Loretta Young's first husband?
12. Who was the actor appearing in This Is the Army who specialized in playing cigar-smoking Greeks during the 40's?
13. Who was the actress appearing in Night unto Night who played the femme fatale in Honeymoon for Three with George Brent and Ann Sheridan?
14. Who was the actor appearing in Brother Rat who later played Mac in the Tiller the Toiler films?
15. Who was the actress appearing in Dark Victory who later played Dr. Christian's nurse-secretary in the film series?

16. Who was the actress appearing in The Angels Wash Their Faces who later became famous as Ma Kettle?

17. Who was the character actor appearing in Brother Rat and a Baby who became famous for his portrayal of the valet, Jeeves?

18. Who was the character actor appearing in An Angel from Texas who later became famous for playing Doc in the TV series "Gunsmoke"?

19. Who was the actress/singer appearing in This Is the Army who was once married to actor Jon Hall?

20. Who was the character actor appearing in Swing Your Lady who was best known for his Irish character-izations and who appeared as the hero's best friend in both One Way Passage and its remake, Till We Meet Again?

Another actor turned politician, George Murphy
(later elected Senator from California), and
Ronald Reagan in a scene from *This Is The Army*
(1943).

RONALD REAGANS "SUPPORTS" QUIZ V

(Score five points for each correct answer.)

1. Who was the character actress appearing in Swing Your Lady who was once married to Hal Wallis?
2. Who was the future star who appeared as a bit player (the movie cashier) in Boy Meets Girl?
3. What actor appearing in Knute Rockne-All American and Santa Fe Trail later married both Michelle Morgan and Ginger Rogers?
4. What relative of Ronald Reagan played the role of Rex Olcott in Tugboat Annie Sails Again?
5. What actor appearing in The Bad Man was the real-life brother of George Sanders?
6. What actress appearing in International Squadron was once known as Jacqueline Wells?
7. Who was the actress appearing in Santa Fe Trail who was crippled in real life and later died as a result of her injuries?
8. What actor appearing in Juke Girl won fame on Broadway and Hollywood portraying Benjamin Franklin in 1776?
9. What character actor appearing in both Desperate Journey and Girls on Probation known for his strong Germanic roles, played Jane Bryan's foster father in the latter film?
10. What character actress appearing in This Is the Army was nominated for Best Supporting Actress in Summer and Smoke?
11. What character actor appearing in Tugboat Annie Sails Again was nominated for Best Supporting Actor in The Alamo?
12. What character actor appearing in International Squadron was also known as "Ukelele Ike"?
13. Who was the character actor appearing in The Voice of the Turtle who was once married to Tallulah Bankhead?
14. Who was the lovely actress appearing in This Is the Army who was once married to John Barrymore?
15. Who was the actor appearing in Cowboy from Brooklyn who later became a major Western star?

76

16. Who was the actress appearing in Swing Your Lady and Boy Meets Girl who later became famous as Hollywood's Blondie?

17. Who was the character actor appearing in Boy Meets Girl who later portrayed Franklin D. Roosevelt in films?

18. Who was the actor appearing in Cowboy from Brooklyn who was once a member of Bing Crosby's trio, the Rhythm Boys?

19. Who was the black character actor appearing in Juke Girl who was best known for his timid (teeth chattering) roles?

20. Who was the Mexican character actor appearing in The Bad Man who later played the Cisco Kid's sidekick?

Ronald Reagan hurrys from his dressing room to his date, Piper Laurie, aged 17. Their destination—the premiere of Francis (the talking mule). Reagan and Laurie were a father/daughter combo in *Louisa*.

RONALD REAGAN "SUPPORTS" QUIZ VI

1. Who was the leading lady of Desperate Journey who also appeared in Kings Row?
2. Who was the Irish comedian appearing in Hollywood Hotel who started in show business with the Three Stooges?
3. What two orchestras and their leaders appeared in Hollywood Hotel?
4. What character actress appearing in Angels Wash Their Faces is best known as the Wicked Witch of the West?
5. What comedian appearing in Naughty but Nice was a former boxer?
6. What character actor appearing in Knute Rockne–All American won an Oscar for How Green Was My Valley?
7. What Irish comedian appearing in Swing Your Lady played the janitor who became top sergeant in Tin Pan Alley?
8. What blonde actress appearing in Hollywood Hotel starred in the Torchy Blane series?
9. What child actor appearing in Knute Rockne–All American and Million Dollar Baby is best known as Tarzan's son?
10. What child actor appearing in Angels Wash Their Faces rose to prominence as the star of Wednesday's Child?
11. What character actor appearing in Knute Rockne–All American and Million Dollar Baby was one of the "Gentle People" in Out of the Fog?
12. What actor appearing in Knute Rockne–All American starred as the Spy Smasher in serials?
13. What comedian appearing in Brother Rat and Cowboy from Brooklyn was also a musician whose middle nickname was "Scat"?
14. What actor appearing in Secret Service of the Air is a member of a famous show-business family and portrayed his father in Lillian Russell?
15. What comedian appearing in Hollywood Hotel was a Country and Western singer and musician with his own group?

16. What black actress appearing in Brother Rat made a great dramatic hit in 1934's Imitation of Life?
17. What wisecracking Irish blonde appearing in This Is the Army played Mary Brian's mother in Hard to Handle?
18. What character actor appearing in Angels Wash Their Faces was the villain in both Gunga Din and Marked Woman?
19. What comedian appearing in Swing Your Lady played Sandor the Strongman in The Great Ziegfield?
20. What character actor appearing in Santa Fe Trail was best known as Ming the Merciless in the Flash Gordon series?

Ronald Reagan in a scene from *Stallion Road* (1947), with Alexis Smith, Zachary Scott and Patti Brady.

WAYNE MORRIS MOVIE QUIZ

(Score five points for each correct answer.)

1. Name the six films in which Wayne Morris and Ronald Reagan appeared together?
2. How many times was Wayne Morris married?
3. How many children did he have?
4. What was his occupation in his "Kid" movies (Kid Galahad, The Kid Comes Back and The Kid from Kokomo)?
5. What was his occupation in The Voice of the Turtle?
6. What was his occupation in I Wanted Wings?
7. What was his occupation in The House Across the Street?
8. What was his occupation in An Angel from Texas?
9. What was his occupation in Brother Rat?
10. Who was his frequent leading lady at Warner Bros.?
11. How many films did he make with her?
12. Who was his leading lady in The Kid from Kokomo?
13. Who was the female star of Kid Galahad?
14. Who was Wayne's leading lady in Kid Galahad?
15. Who was the female star of Deep Valley?
16. Who was the female star of Bad Men from Missouri?
17. Who was the female star of Johnny One-Eye?
18. Who was the male star of Johnny One-Eye?
19. Who was the male star of The Time of Your Life?
20. Who was the female star of A Kiss in the Dark?

ALAN HALE MOVIE QUIZ

(Score five points for each correct answer.)

1. Name the five films in which Alan Hale and Ronald Reagan appeared together.
2. He made 13 films starring his oft-times drinking pal. Who was this star?
3. Which sister did he marry in The Sisters?
4. Who was his wife in They Drive by Night?
5. Who was his "best-gal" friend in Stella Dallas?
6. Who was the dancing star of On Your Toes?
7. Who were the two stars of Thin Ice?
8. Who played the title role in Babbitt?
9. Who played his wife?
10. Who played the title role in The Little Minister?
11. Who was the leading lady in that film?
12. Who played the title role in Adventures of Marco Polo?
13. Who played the title role in Tugboat Annie Sails Again?
14. Who played the title role in The Great Mr. Nobody?
15. Who played the title role in Gentleman Jim?
16. Who played the title role in The Man in the Iron Mask?
17. Who played the title roles in Four Men and a Prayer?
18. Who played the title role in The Sin of Madelon Claudet?
19. Who played the title role in Susan Lennox-Her Fall and Rise?
20. Who played the title role in The Match King?

DICK POWELL MOVIE QUIZ

(Score five points for each correct answer.)

1. Name the four films in which Dick Powell and Ronald Reagan appeared together.
2. Name Dick Powell's two actress-wives.
3. How many children did he have?
4. What tap-dancing star was his frequent co-star?
5. How many films did they make together?
6. Name those films.
7. Where is "Flirtation Walk"?
8. What was the film in which he first appeared as a tough guy?
9. What fictitious detective did he portray in that film?
10. What was the title of the only Western that he made?
11. In what film did he play a Mountie?
12. Which film of his dealt with a plot to assassinate President Lincoln?
13. What were the two films he made with Mary Martin?
14. What was the one film he made with Dorothy Lamour?
15. In what film did he sing "I Only Have Eyes for You"?
16. In what film did he sing "I'll String Along with You"?
17. In what film did he sing "Shuffle Off to Buffalo"?
18. In what film did he sing "I've Got My Love to Keep Me Warm"?
19. In what film did he sing "Honeymoon Hotel"?
20. In what film did he sing "Mr. and Mrs. Is the Name"?

DORIS DAY MOVIE QUIZ

(Score five points for each correct answer.)

1. Name the three films in which Doris Day and Ronald Reagan appeared together.
2. In which film were they co-starred?
3. What role did Doris Day play in this film?
4. What malady did Ronald Reagan contract in this film?
5. For what ball team did Ronald Reagan play?
6. What year did this ball team win the World Series pennant?
7. What position did Ronald Reagan play in this film?
8. How many games did this player win during his career?
9. Who were Doris Day's two male co-stars in It's a Great Feeling?
10. In 1951 Doris played the wife of a well-known American songwriter. What was the film?
11. Who played the songwriter?
12. What was the name of this songwriter?
13. In 1953 she played a famous real-life Western woman. What was the film?
14. In 1955 she played the life story of a well-known singer. What was the film?
15. Who was this singer?
16. Who was Doris Day's co-star in this film?
17. For what film was Doris Day nominated for an Oscar?
18. Who was her co-star in this film?
19. How many years was Doris Day a top box-office star?
20. What were these years?

PAT O'BRIEN MOVIE QUIZ

(Score five points for each correct answer.)

1. Name the four films in which Pat O'Brien and Ronald Reagan appeared together.
2. Pat O'Brien and James Cagney have both been persuaded to come out of retirement to co-star again. In what film?
3. How many films did Pat O'Brien and James Cagney make together?
4. What was the name of their 1934 film?
5. What was the name of their first 1935 film?
6. What was the name of their second 1935 film?
7. What was the name of their third 1935 film?
8. What was the name of their first 1938 film?
9. What was the name of their second 1938 film?
10. What was the name of their first 1940 film?
11. What was the name of their second 1940 film?
12. How many times did Pat O'Brien play a priest and what were the films?
13. In 1948 he made a film with an unusual premise which had a color in the title. What was the film?
14. What were the two films in which he played a telephone lineman?
15. What was the film in which he played a Hollywood scriptwriter?
16. What were the films in which he played a Hollywood press agent?
17. What were the films in which he played a Broadway press agent?
18. What was the film in which he played an auctioneer?
19. What was the film in which he played an oil worker in the U.S.?
20. What was the film in which he played an oil worker in China?

Ronald Reagan as Notre Dame's greatest football player, George Gipp. Here Ronald discusses the film, *Life of Knute Rockne,* with Pat O'Brien who played the title role.

ANN SHERIDAN MOVIE QUIZ

(Score five points for each correct answer.)

1. Name the four films in which Ann Sheridan and Ronald Reagan appeared together.
2. What was Ann Sheridan's name in Kings Row?
3. Who wrote the novel on which Kings Row was based?
4. Who played the part of Louise Gordon, the girl who loved Ronald Reagan throughout Kings Row?
5. Who played Louise Gordon's cruel parents?
6. What was Ronald Reagan's five-word question in Kings Row, whence he derived the title of his autobiography?
7. Who was the male lead of Naughty but Nice?
8. What was Ann Sheridan's profession in Naughty but Nice?
9. In what film did Ann Sheridan sing "You're Just an Angel in Disguise"?
10. In what film did Ann Sheridan sing "Just Like a Gypsy"?
11. In what film did Ann Sheridan sing "Love Isn't Born, It's Made"?
12. What role did she play in The Man Who Came to Dinner?
13. What role did she play in Shine On, Harvest Moon?
14. Name Ann Sheridan's three actor husbands.
15. Who was Ann Sheridan's leading man in George Washington Slept Here?
16. Who was Ann Sheridan's leading man in I Married a Male War Bride?
17. Who were Ann Sheridan's two female co-stars in The Doughnuts?
18. Who was Ann Sheridan's leading man in City for Conquest?
19. Who was Ann Sheridan's leading man in Edge of Darkness?
20. Who was Ann Sheridan's leading man in They Drive by Night?

RHONDA FLEMING MOVIE QUIZ

(Score five points for each correct answer.)

1. Name the four films in which Rhonda Fleming and Ronald Reagan appeared together.
2. Who was the third star of The Last Outpost?
3. Who was the third star of Tennessee's Partner?
4. Where did Tropic Zone take place?
5. What was the setting?
6. What was the 1946 Hitchcock film that brought Rhonda Fleming to Hollywood's attention?
7. What was the 1947 film in which she was co-starred for the first time?
8. Who was her co-star?
9. This was a remake of what 1937 film?
10. Who had the leads in the 1937 film?
11. In 1949 she was the leading lady in two films with Paramount's two top male stars. What were the films and who were the male stars?
12. In 1957 she appeared in The Buster Keaton Story. Who played the title role?
13. In 1959 she appeared in Alias Jesse James. Who played the title role?
14. In 1958 she played the evil sister of the star of Home Before Dark. Who was the star who was nominated for an Oscar for that role?
15. Who was her leading man in Pony Express?
16. Who was her leading man in Gun Glory?
17. Who was her leading man in Jivaro?
18. Who was her leading man in Crosswinds?
19. Who was her leading man in The Redhead and the Cowboy?
20. Who was her leading man in Yankee Pasha?

PRISCILLA LANE MOVIE QUIZ

(Score five points for each correct answer.)

1. Name the four films in which Priscilla Lane and Ronald Reagan appeared together.
2. What minor role did Ronald Reagan play in Cowboy from Brooklyn?
3. What was Ronald Reagan's profession in Million Dollar Baby?
4. What was Ronald Reagan's profession in Brother Rat?
5. In 1952 Brother Rat was remade by Warner Bros. as a musical. What was the name of this remake?
6. Who was the male star of the remake?
7. In 1942 Priscilla Lane co-starred in a well-known Hitchcock wartime drama. What was the title of this film?
8. Who was her co-star?
9. Who were the two actress sisters of Priscilla Lane?
10. What is their real family name?
11. What is the first name of the fourth sister?
12. Who played the fourth sister in the series about the Lemp Sisters?
13. Name the three films in this series?
14. Who played the father in this series?
15. Who played the grandmother in this series?
16. In what activity did the Lemp family indulge?
17. Who was Priscilla's leading man in Arsenic and Old Lace?
18. Who was her leading man in The Meanest Man in Town?
19. Who was her leading man in The Roaring Twenties?
20. Who was the man she married in The Roaring Twenties?

Priscilla Lane and Wayne Morris (couple on the right) were supported in the 1938 classic, *Brother Rat*, by Jane Wyman and her future husband, Ronald Reagan.

EDDIE ALBERT MOVIE QUIZ

(Score five points for each correct answer.)

1. Name the three films in which Eddie Albert and Ronald Reagan appeared together.
2. Name the 1961 film in which Eddie Albert appeared and Ronald Reagan did the narration.
3. Name the two films for which Eddie Albert was nominated as Best Supporting Actor.
4. What was Eddie Albert's name in the two Brother Rat films?
5. What was Eddie Albert's name in the Four Daughter's series?
6. Which of the Lemp girls did Eddie Albert marry in that series?
7. Which of the Lemp girls did Frank McHugh marry in that series?
8. Which of the Lemp girls did Jeffrey Lynn marry in that series?
9. Which of the Lemp girls did Dick Foran marry in that series.
10. Which of these couples had twins in Four Mothers?
11. Who played the part of Mickey Borden in Four Daughters?
12. Who was Eddie Albert's leading lady in Ladies Day?
13. Who was his leading lady in Lady Bodyguard?
14. Who was his leading lady in The Great Mr. Nobody?
15. What two real-life people was Beloved Infidel about?
16. Who was nominated for an Oscar for Smash up-The Story of a Woman?
17. Who was nominated for an Oscar for Roman Holiday?
18. Which Oscar-winning actress was the female lead in You Gotta Stay Happy?
19. Which Oscar-winning actor was the male lead in You Gotta Stay Happy?
20. Which Oscar-winning actor was the male lead in You're in the Navy Now?

HUMPHREY BOGART MOVIE QUIZ

(Score five points for each correct answer.)

1. Name the three films in which Humphrey Bogart and Ronald Reagan appeared together.
2. How many times was Humphrey Bogart married?
3. They were all actresses. Can you name them?
4. How many children did he have?
5. For what good friend was his daughter named?
6. After a dismal early Hollywood career, what stage play in 1935 brought him fame and back to Hollywood for its filming?
7. What was his name in this play and film?
8. In what film did he play Duke Verne?
9. In what film did he play Baby Face Martin?
10. In what film did he play Charlie Allnut?
11. In what film did he play Captain Queeg?
12. In what film did he play Philip Marlowe?
13. In what film did he play Rick Blaine?
14. In what film did he play Gloves Donahue?
15. In what film did he play "Mad Dog" Roy Earle?
16. In what film did he play Whip McCord?
17. In what film did he play Rocks Valentine?
18. In what film did he play Turkey Morgan?
19. For what film did he win his Oscar?
20. For which two other films was he nominated?

JANE BRYAN MOVIE QUIZ

(Score five points for each correct answer.)

1. Name the three films in which Jane Bryan and Ronald Reagan appeared together.
2. In what two films did she play Bette Davis' sister?
3. In what film did she play Bette Davis' illegitimate daughter?
4. In what film did she play Edward G. Robinson's sister?
5. In what film did she play Edward G. Robinson's daughter?
6. In what film did she play Kay Francis' daughter?
7. In what film did she play Charley Grapewin's granddaughter?
8. Who was her co-star in We Are Not Alone?
9. Who played his wife in that film?
10. Who played Jane Bryan's husband in Brother Rat and Brother Rat and a Baby?
11. Who were the two male stars of Each Dawn I Die?
12. Who were the two male stars of Invisible Stripes?
13. What do these two films have in common?
14. Who were the four male leads in These Glamour Girls?
15. Who were the five female leads in These Glamour Girls?
16. In The Case of the Black Cat, who played Perry Mason?
17. Who played Della Street in that film?
18. Who was the child star in The Captain's Kid?
19. Who was the Captain?
20. In addition to Bette and Jane, who were the four other females featured as "hostesses" in Marked Woman?

PATRICIA NEAL MOVIE QUIZ

(Score five points for each correct answer.)

1. Name the three films in which Patricia Neal and Ronald Reagan appeared together.
2. In which Ronald Reagan film did Patricia Neal make her screen debut?
3. What was Patricia Neal's profession in The Hasty Heart?
4. Name the film for which Patricia Neal won her Oscar?
5. Name the other film for which she was nominated for an Oscar.
6. Who were the other two female leads in Three Secrets?
7. Whom did Patricia Neal marry and what is his profession?
8. How many children do they have?
9. What play on Broadway brought her to the attention of Hollywood?
10. What role did she portray in this Broadway play?
11. Who played this role in the film version?
12. Who wrote this play?
13. Who wrote the novel The Fountainhead which became an early Patricia Neal film?
14. Who wrote the story on which Patricia Neal's film The Breaking Point, was based?
15. Who was her leading man in Bright Leaf?
16. Who was her leading man in Weekend with Father?
17. Who was her leading man in Raton Pass?
18. Who was her leading man in Washington Story?
19. Who was her leading man in The Subject Was Roses?
20. Who wrote the novel Breakfast at Tiffany's, in which Patricia Neal appeared?

Scene from Warner Bros. *Desperate Journey* (1942), with Errol Flynn, Ronald Reagan, Alan Hale and Arthur Kennedy.

Wallace Beery, Lionel Barrymore, Laraine Day and Ronald Reagan star in scene from the 1941 MGM movie, *The Bad Man*.

Ronald Reagan speaks at the 1943 Hollywood Academy Awards ceremonies at Hollywood's Chinese Theater. George Jessel and Donald Crisp are pictured in the background.

RONALD REAGAN FILMS, CROSS-SECTION QUIZ I

(Score five points for each correct answer.)

1. What was Ronald Reagan's first film?
2. What was his last film?
3. What is the title of the 1961 film in which Ronald Reagan does not appear, but narrates?
4. Tropic Zone, Hong Kong, The ___ Heart, International Squadron, Prisoner of War and Desperate Journey are six Ronald Reagan films that ___ thing in common. What is that?
5. What is the one Ronald Reagan film with a one-word title?
6. What do the characters that Reagan played in Santa Fe Trail, The Winning Team and Knute Rockne–All American have in common?
7. In terms of photography, what sets The Killers, Tennessee's Partner, Cattle Queen of Montana, Law and Order, Tropic Zone, Hong Kong, She's Working Her Way Through College, The Last Outpost, It's a Great Feeling and This Is the Army apart from Ronald Reagan's other pictures?
8. The greatest age difference between Ronald Reagan and one of his leading ladies was 18 years. Who was she and what was the film?
9. What do Tennessee's Partner, Cattle Queen of Montana, Santa Fe Trail, The Last Outpost, Law and Order and The Bad Man have in common?
10. On what type of vessel is Ronald Reagan stationed in Hellcats of the Navy?
11. Ronald Reagan's 1964 film, The Killers, was a remake of what 1946 film starring Burt Lancaster, Ava Gardner and Edmund O'Brien?
12. Ronald Reagan appears in both Brother Rat (1938) and its 1940 sequel. What's its title?
13. Tugboat Annie Sails Again, a 1940 film in which Ronald Reagan appears, was a sequel to a film made four years before he entered the movies. What is the title of the original Tugboat Annie film?
14. What is the title of a 1963 film starring Susan Hayward that was a remake of Dark Victory (1939), a Bette Davis film in which Ronald Reagan appears?

96

15. What 1938 film in which Ronald Reagan appears provided Susan Hayward with her first meaty role as a Warners starlet?

16. What sets The Killers, The Young Doctors, Hellcats of the Navy, Tennessee's Partner, Cattle Queen of Montana, Prisoner of War, Law and Order, Tropic Zone, Hong Kong, The Last Outpost, The Badman and Louisa apart from other Ronald Reagan films?

17. What was the one film that Ronald Reagan made for Columbia?

18. What was the one film that he made for United Artists?

19. What Ronald Reagan film was originally shot for television, but released in theaters when deemed too violent for the small screen?

20. What was the first film that Ronald Reagan made when he got out of the U.S. Army?

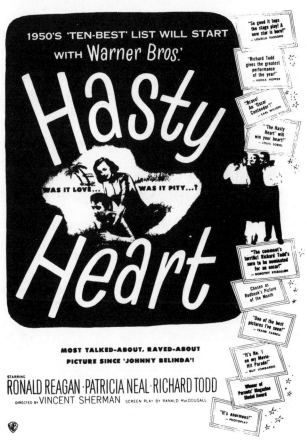

Movie ad for Warner Bros. *Hasty Heart.*

RONALD REAGAN FILMS, CROSS-SECTION QUIZ II

(Score five points for each correct answer.)

1. What do the characters portrayed by Ronald Reagan in The Killers, Tennessee's Partner, Knute Rockne-All American and International Squadron have in common?
2. What do Sergeant Murphy and Bedtime for Bonzo have in common?
3. What do Brother Rat, Brother Rat and a Baby, Stallion Road, The Voice of the Turtle, Hellcats of the Navy and Cattle Queen of Montana have in common?
4. What activity that Ronald Reagan particularly enjoys did he get to do in Sergeant Murphy, Santa Fe Trail, Stallion Road, The Last Outpost, Cattle Queen of Montana and Tennessee's Partner?
5. Juke Girl and Night unto Night are two very different Ronald Reagan films that have one thing in common. What's that?
6. Tropic Zone is set in Central America. The Hasty Heart in Burma. Aside from the fact that they are set in foreign locales half a world apart, what do they have in common vis-a-vis geography?
7. What do Knute Rockne-All American, Tugboat Annie Sails Again, That Hagen Girl, John Loves Mary, Louisa and Tennessee's Partner have in common?
8. What do Hollywood Hotel, Cowboy from Brooklyn, Hell's Kitchen, An Angel from Texas, Hong Kong and Cattle Queen of Montana have in common?
9. In what two films did Ronald Reagan work with the Bowery Boys?
10. What two Ronald Reagan films have titles that refer to royalty?
11. What three Ronald Reagan films have the name of a state in their titles?
12. "A boy meets a juke girl named Hagen, who is on probation from Jones Beach." The preceding nonsense sentence should help you recall the five films that Ronald Reagan made with the word "girl" in the title. Name all five.
13. What do Brother Rat, Knute Rockne-All American, Bedtime for Bonzo and She's Working Her Way Through College have in common?

14. Even more specifically, what do <u>Bedtime for Bonzo</u> and <u>She's Working Her Way Through College</u> have in common?

15. What two Ronald Reagan films contain in their titles the names of immortal beings attendant upon God?

16. What do <u>Sergeant Murphy</u>, <u>This Is the Army</u>, <u>The Voice of the Turtle</u>, <u>John Loves Mary</u>, <u>The Hasty Heart</u>, <u>The Last Outpost</u> and <u>Santa Fe Trail</u> have in common?

17. What two celebrated scenes from <u>Knute Rockne-All American</u> are cut from all TV presentations of that film because of legal complications with the real-life family of the character portrayed by Ronald Reagan?

18. What 1938 Ronald Reagan film was remade in 1952 as <u>About Face</u> with Gordon MacRae and Eddie Bracken?

19. What is the title of the 1937 film from which Ronald Reagan's scenes were totally deleted?

20. Ronald Reagan played a lot of soldier boys. In all but one he served the flag of the United States. In what film did he play an officer at war with the United States and what was the country?

A Ronald Reagan studio publicity head shot (autographed).

RONALD REAGAN FILMS, CROSS SECTION QUIZ III

(Score five points for each correct answer.)

1. What is the one film in which Ronald Reagan played a "heavy" or bad guy?
2. What Ronald Reagan film has the longest title?
3. What was the last film that Ronald Reagan made for Warner Bros.?
4. What was the first film that Ronald Reagan made for a studio other than Warner Bros.?
5. At the end of one Ronald Reagan film a man is hanged and someone comments, "So perish all such enemies of the Union!" Who is hanged and what's the film?
6. What was it about That Hagen Girl that embarrassed Ronald Reagan?
7. In what film, co-starring Ronald Reagan, does Errol Flynn say, "Now for Australia and a crack at the Japs"?
8. Although Ronald Reagan made a number of Westerns, Indians are pivotal to the plot in only two. Which two?
9. Although Ronald Reagan loved westerns, he didn't get a chance to make a real one until he had been in the movie business for 14 years. Not including The Bad Man or Santa Fe Trail, what was Ronald Reagan's first Western?
10. From what affliction does the character portrayed by Ronald Reagan in The Winning Team suffer?
11. The Hasty Heart is set in Burma. But where was it filmed?
12. What do the characters portrayed by Ronald Reagan in She's Working Her Way Through College, Louisa and The Winning Team have in common vis-a-vis a legal commitment?
13. An Angel from Texas refers to what type of angel?
14. Ronald Reagan's films do not go back very far in history. Of all Ronald Reagan films which has the earliest historical setting?
15. What is the one film in which Ronald Reagan has both a daughter and a son? Who played the daughter?
16. What is the one film in which Ronald Reagan has a single child and who played him?

17. What two Ronald Reagan films contain in their titles the name of a nether region reputed to be unbearably hot?

18. On the set of one of Ronald Reagan's Westerns, his dauntless leading lady so impressed the Blackfoot Indians that they made her a blood sister and dubbed her Princess Many Victories. Who is she?

19. Movie stills from Ronald Reagan's Westerns reveal the fact that he's left-nanded. What did he wear that inescapably revealed his lefthandedness?

20. In what film did Reagan play a real-life person who was named after a former U.S. president and what was the name of the person he played?

Here's the *first* story! Here's the *furious* story! Here's the *screaming* story of the RAF's daredevil Aces in Exile. From every conquered corner of the globe they come—avenging 'angels' sky-writing their heroic history!

Movie ad for *International Squadron*.

RONALD REAGAN FILM DATES QUIZ

Listed on the left below are 20 films in whch Ronald reagan played. Listed on the right are the dates of those films and the studios for which they were made. Match them.

(Score five points for each correct answer.)

1.	Knute Rockne–All American	A.	1938, WB
2.	Tennessee's Partner	B.	1942, WB
3.	Love Is on the Air	C.	1940, WB
4.	The Voice of the Turtle	D.	1951, Universal
5.	The Killers	E.	1952, WB
6.	Cattle Queen of Montana	F.	1949, WB
7.	The Bad Man	G.	1964, Universal
8.	Juke Girl	H.	1950, WB
9.	John Loves Mary	I.	1943, WB
10.	Hellcats of the Navy	J.	1953, Paramount
11.	Storm Warning	K.	1957, Columbia
12.	This Is the Army	L.	1937, WB
13.	Prisoner of War	M.	1947, WB
14.	Bedtime for Bonzo	N.	1941, MGM
15.	Law and Order	O.	1954, RKO
16.	Tropic Zone	P.	1954, MGM
17.	Hong Kong	Q.	1955, RKO
18.	Going Places	R.	1953, Universal
19.	She's Working Her Way Through College	S.	1939, WB
		T.	1951, Paramount
20.	Dark Victory		

Ronald Reagan playing the heavy in his last film, *The Killers,* (Universal, 1964).

CAPSULE SUMMARY QUIZ I OF RONALD REAGAN FILMS

(Score five points for each correct answer.)

1. In what film is Ronald Reagan a cocky, smart-aleck American living in England who finally redeems himself in a serial combat?

2. In what film does a teenage girl who believes herself to be Ronald Reagan's illegitimate daughter wind up in his arms when she finds out otherwise?

3. In what film does Ronald Reagan make a living throwing fast-balls, curves, sliders and sinkers?

4. In what film does Ronnie Reagan fight the bad guys to save Rhonda Fleming's banana plantation?

5. In what film does soldier Reagan share a Manhattan apartment with a wide-eyed, warm-hearted actress?

6. In what film does veterinarian Reagan vie with novelist Zachary Scott for the affections of ranch-owner Alexis Smith?

7. In what film is Ronald Reagan a fruit-picker who gets involved in a murder case?

8. In the last of Ronald Reagan's Secret Service films, he again played Brass Bancroft, this time preventing enemy agents from purloining secret plans. What's the name of the film?

9. In what comedy film does professor Reagan play daddy to man's closest cousin in the interests of science?

10. In what film are Ronald Reagan and Bruce Bennett brothers on opposite sides of the Civil War who team up out West to help ward off an Indian attack?

11. What Ronald Reagan film entails the trials and tribulations of a naive girl when she suddenly inherits a lot of money?

12. In what film is Ronald Reagan a dying scientist who finds love with an emotionally disturbed woman?

13. In what film, set in an Army hospital in Burma, does Ronald Reagan befriend an embittered Scottish soldier who has only a short time to live?

14. In what World War II film does Ronald Reagan command a submarine, engage in naval combat and woo pretty nurse Nancy Davis?

15. In what film are Errol Flynn and Ronald Reagan downed American pilots trapped behind enemy lines in World War II Germany?

16. In what film in which Ronald Reagan appears is Spring Byington, trying to become a December bride, undecided as to whom she should marry?

17. What 1937 film in which Ronald Reagan appears features Dick Powell, an all-star cast and the song "Hooray for Hollywood"?

18. In what pre-Civil War Western that seems undecided as to which side of the slavery issue it's on does Ronald Reagan play George Armstrong Custer to Errol Flynn's Jeb Stuart and Raymond Massey's John Brown?

19. What 1938 film, starring Wayne Morris, Eddie Albert and Ronald Reagan, portrays the zany escapades of a cadet trio at the Virginia Military Institute?

20. What film in which Ronald Reagan appears stars Bette Davis as a dying socialite, Geraldine Fitzgerald as her loyal friend, George Brent as a brain surgeon and Humphrey Bogart as an Irish stable-keeper?

Movie ad for Warner Bros. *That Hagen Girl* starring Ronald Reagan, Shirley Temple (eventual United States Ambassador to the United Nations) and Rory Calhoun.

CAPSULE SUMMARY QUIZ II OF RONALD REAGAN FILMS

(Score five points for each correct answer.)

1. In what film does Ronald Reagan save the job of a lovable old lady who makes her living going down to the sea in an unshapely ship?

2. In a 1949 film, Jack Carson (playing himself) assures Judy Adams (played by Doris Day) that he can make her a star and has her pose as pregnant to obtain the sympathy of Dennis Morgan (playing himself), whom Carson wants to direct in a picture. It goes on from there until Judy, eschewing a film career, goes home and marries her childhood sweetheart, Jeffrey Bushfinkle (Errol Flynn). A number of other Hollywood stars, including Jane Wyman and Ronald Reagan, appear as themselves in this picture. What's its title?

3. In what film, set in an exotic locale, is adventurer Reagan tempted to steal a Chinese orphan's valuable antique before finally seeing the error of his ways?

4. In what off-beat Western does cowpoke Reagan become a pal to tinhorn gambler John Payne?

5. In what modern-day Western in which Ronald Reagan appears is blustery Mexican bandit Wallace Beery loyal to an erstwhile buddy, ranch-owner Lionel Barrymore?

6. In 1939 Ronald Reagan made two films with the Dead End Kids. In which one did he play a district attorney's son in love with Ann Sheridan, a poor girl trying to keep her kid brother out of trouble?

7. In what Dead End Kids film are Ronald Reagan and Margaret Lindsay dedicated social workers?

8. What film in which Ronald Reagan appears is a zany Hollywood satire about two screenwriters and their attempts to hit the big time?

9. Soldier Ronald Reagan loves fellow-American Pat Neal but marries English girl Virginia Field so she can come to America and marry Jack Carson, who it turns out is already married. But as Virginia Field's first husband, Wayne Morris, turns up alive and well, she is not legally married to soldier Reagan who winds up in the arms of Pat Neal. What's the name of this 1949 film comedy?

10. Ginger Rogers witnesses a Ku Klux Klan murder and is threatened by that organization until prosecuting attorney Ronald Reagan puts slimy killer Steve Cochran behind bars. What's the film?

11. In what film does college football star Ronald Reagan die prematurely, inspiring his coach, Pat O'Brien, to exhort his players to "win one for the Gipper"?

12. In what remake of The Male Animal is Ronald Reagan a mild-mannered college professor befuddled by the fact that one of his pupils is a burlesque queen who has aspirations of being a writer but is about to get expelled from school because of her profession?

13. What first-rate film in which Ronald Reagan has a strong supporting role is set in small-town America before World War I and has been referred to as a forerunner of Peyton Place?

14. In what film in which Ronald Reagan appears does prim music professor Dick Powell write a hit song that complicates his life and forces him to change his personality?

15. In what film does artist Ronald Reagan encounter the girl of his dreams at the ocean shore?

16. In what film does Ronald Reagan help a lady hold on to her ranch despite hungry land-grabbers and hostile Indians?

17. In what film in which Ronald Reagan plays an assistant to show-biz promoter Pat O'Brien is tenderfoot Dick Powell obliged to prove that he is a genuine cowboy lest he lose his job as a Western balladeer on the radio?

18. In what film, based on a true story, is Ronald Reagan a cavalry private devoted to his gun-shy steed who finally wins acclaim in horse shows, including England's Grand National?

19. In what Western is Ronald Reagan a Tombstone-taming marshal who wants to retire to a ranch and wed Dorothy Malone, but first feels obliged to take on the bad guys in a town called Cottonwood?

20. In what film is Ronald Reagan an Army officer who upon hearing that American soldiers are being brain-washed and tortured by their North Korean captors becomes a P.O.W. to verify that fact?

THERE IS A STORY ABOUT A TOWN CALLED KINGS ROW

All knew it but none talked about it — *except in whispers.*

You'll live strange experiences you never dreamed could come into your life as the screen captures each ecstatic moment and every secret longing of these shadowed characters. Here is screen great-ness, truly!

ANN SHERIDAN
as tempting 'RANDY'

ROBERT CUMMINGS
as handsome 'PARRIS'

RONALD REAGAN
as irresistible 'DRAKE'

BETTY FIELD
as stormy 'CASSIE'

KINGS ROW

WHERE EVERY HEART CONCEALED A SECRET SIN

To be long remembered for the best-seller it was —for the magnificent film it is!

Directed by
SAM WOOD
of 'Mr. Chips' and
'Kitty' Foyle' fame!

WARNER BROS! NEW SUCCESS, with CHARLES COBURN
Claude Rains · Judith Anderson · Nancy Coleman

The Screen Play is superbly adapted by Casey Robinson from the Novel by Henry Bellamann • Music by Erich Wolfgang Korngold

Now at the Astor Theatre in New York duplicating the success of 'Sergeant York', the Warner Bros. picture that preceded it there. AT YOUR THEATRE SOON. Check the manager for exact date.

APRIL, 1942

Movie ad for Warner Bros., *Kings Row,* (1942).

Congratulations Errol Flynn

FOR YOUR VERY, VERY BEST WARNER BROS. PICTURE!

What a list of hits he has behind him! Yet for excitement unsurpassed, for pace unparalleled, for action beyond compare - - for everything that makes an adventure-picture a life-long adventure for moviegoers, the top of the list is

ERROL FLYNN
thrillingly, stirringly teamed with fandom's favorite
RONALD REAGAN
to lead a 5-man Commando mission in a devastating dash to Berlin and back!

DESPERATE JOURNEY
TO BE SEEN THIS MONTH!
(To be sure of the date check with your theatre)

WHEN YOUR JOHNNY COMES MARCHING HOME THESE ARE THE STORIES HE'LL TELL

She handled the Nazis her own way —a woman's way!

September is SALUTE TO OUR HEROES month at all movie theatres! Buy a War Bond to honor every mother's son in Service!

With NANCY COLEMAN · RAYMOND MASSEY
Alan Hale · Arthur Kennedy · Directed by RAOUL WALSH
Original Screen Play by Arthur T. Horman
PRODUCED BY HAL B. WALLIS
Music by Max Steiner

OCTOBER, 1942

Promotional piece for Warner Bros. *Desperate Journey*.

RONALD REAGAN FILM COMMENTARY QUIZ

Can you identify those films of his to which Ronald Reagan was referring in the following quotes?

(Score five points for each corect answer.)

1. "There is room for only one discovery in a picture. Eddie Albert stole the honors and deservedly so."
2. "We drove up the beautiful Monterey Peninsula, to the 11th Cavalry, where all the outdoor shooting would take place. This was a little more homelike and familiar to me than the sound stage at the studio. Playing a cavalryman, surrounded by regular Army personnel, was reminiscent of my last few years at Fort Des Moines."
3. "The very next scene called for me to make an entrance in Grand Central Station, face a battery of the press and, complete with straw hat and cane, do a carnival shill act introducing our cowboy discovery."
4. "Came the moment on the screen when I said to Shirley, 'I love you,' and the entire audience cried, en masse, 'Oh, no!' I sat huddled in the darkness until I was sure the lobby would be empty. You couldn't have gotten me to face that audience for a million bucks. Before release the line was edited out of the picture, leaving us with a kind of oddball finish in which we climb on a train-Shirley carrying a bouquet-and leave town. You are left to guess as to whether we are married, just traveling together, or did I adopt her?"
5. "Our 'Spitfire' was a doctored-up Ryan monoplane that didn't even have retractable gear."
6. "I discovered how nervous fatigue can creep up on you. On the night shift, going to work at 6 PM, we shot night exteriors until sun up for 38 nights. With all the misconceptions about pampered stars, none is so far afield as the belief that physical discomfort isn't tolerated." (Referring to a 1942 film with Ann Sheridan.)
7. "I had been warned about Beery, but no one had said anything about Barrymore. Let me make one thing plain-it was a great honor to work with him, and I'm glad I had the opportunity."
8. "A lot of acting is imitation anyway, and I became pretty good, as long as the piano remained silent. For

a while there I almost convinced myself I could play."

9. "It was the springboard that bounced me into a wider variety of parts in pictures. It's true, I got some unmerited criticism from sports writers."

10. "I've always regretted that the studio insisted we not use the word of "epilepsy", although we tried to get the idea across. The trouble was that a frank naming the illness would have the ring of truth, whereas ducking it made some critics accuse us of inventing something to whitewash his alcoholism."

11. "I knew the script was hopeless, but there was a little matter of a debt of gratitude because they had given me The Last Outpost when no one else would let me get outdoors." (Referring to a 1953 film with Rhonda Fleming.)

12. "The picture should have done better. Every torture scene and incident was based on actual happenings documented in official Army records. Unfortunately, production and release were both rushed, with the idea the picture should come out while the headlines were hot."

13. "But time after time, Freddie, like the rest of us, was so capitvated that he'd forget and start to direct Bonzo as he did the human cast members."

14. "After all, it was a basis for believing in ghosts when you stopped to think he could have drifted in on any part of 4000 miles of coastline."

15. "That's exactly how the play ends, but you first have to keep the audience laughing for two hours or you have a one-reel short. We did pretty well." (Referring to a 1949 film.)

16. "It was a long, hard schedule and my first experience, I suppose, with an acting chore that got down inside and kind of wrung me out."

17. "I still insist there is only one way to play a scene and that is simply and with great sincerity. Our director hit the ceiling. He demanded, 'Do you think you are playing the leading man? George has that part, you know.' "

18. What follows is not a Ronald Reagan quote in reference to a specific film, but to a certain film genre. What type of films did he have in mind when he remarked that they are set in an era "recent enough to be real and old enough to be romantic"?

STARS BORN IN ILLINOIS QUIZ

Ronald Reagan was born in the state of Illinois. So were 20 other Hollywood stars, brief descriptions of whom are given below. Identify the stars.

(Score five points for each correct answer.)

1. Bing of Brother Rat.
2. Won Supporting Actress Oscar for Written on the Wind.
3. The ultimate Tarzan of the talkies.
4. Won Supporting Actress Oscar for The Great Lie.
5. Oldest brother in Seven Brothers, also played Frank Butler and Gaylord Ravenol.
6. Nellie Forbush of the film musical.
7. Madge of Picnic, also mistress of Pyewacket.
8. Two-time Best Supporting Actor, who also portrayed George S. Kaufman.
9. "Love in Bloom" violinist, owned a Maxwell car.
10. Former novitiate who married a top film star.
11. Marcus Welby, M.D.
12. Made brilliant comeback as Norma Desmond.
13. That "Absent-Minded Professor."
14. Moses, Ben-Hur, Andrew Jackson.
15. Won Supporting Actress Oscar for All The King's Men.
16. Knute Rockne.
17. Down-and-out boxer in The Set-Up.
18. Doris Day's and Carol Burnett's favorite playmate.
19. "Golden Boy" who won an Oscar as a P.O.W.
20. Juvenile who matured into a song-and-dance man, played Buster Keaton.

Ronald Reagan and Barbara Stanwyck in a scene from *Cattle Queen of Montana*.

Ronald Reagan with Errol Flynn, Alan Hale, Ronald Sinclair and Raymond Massey in *Desperate Journey*.

STARS BORN IN CALIFORNIA QUIZ I

Ronald Reagan's adopted state is California, where he served two terms as Governor and where he owns two homes. Listed below are clues to 20 stars who were born in that state. Identify them.

(Score five points for each correct answer.)

1. Capt. Ahab, Captain Newman, M.D., The Man in the Gray Flannel Suit.
2. Little Miss Marker, Mrs. Black.
3. Buffalo Bill Cody, Sullivan.
4. Our Miss Brooks of the wisecracks.
5. Jezebel's aunt, Mrs. Wiggs, Mrs. Hadley.
6. Underwater TV star.
7. Scatterbrained wife of George.
8. Mexican character actor, noted chef.
9. His father was master of horror make-up in silents.
10. Noted for exasperated businessmen, Gracie Allen's TV neighbor.
11. Played Klansman in a Reagan film.
12. Skippy.
13. Original Flash Gordon and Buck Rogers.
14. Pinky, Margie, Peggy, also one of "Three Wives."
15. One of "Two Girls" with June Allyson and "A Sailor."
16. Joe Palooka of the 1930s.
17. Reagan's four-time leading lady in adventure films.
18. Won Supporting Actress Oscar for The Bad and the Beautiful.
19. A killer in Rope, a near-victim in Strangers on a Train.
20. Gable's part-time girlfriend for many years.

A 1940s studio glamour shot of Ronald Reagan.

STARS BORN IN CALIFORNIA QUIZ II

See Quiz I. (Score five points for each correct answer.)

1. Male star of The Hurricane, also TV's Ramar.
2. Comic character noted for his "slow burn."
3. The first Mrs. Tony Curtis, mother of Jamie Lee.
4. Reagan's wife in Bedtime for Bonzo.
5. The blonde sex symbol of the 1950s and 60s.
6. Robert Wagner's leading lady in Beneath the Twelve Mile Reef.
7. Star of Brother Rat and The Quarterback.
8. Bus Stop hero who married Hope Lange.
9. Capt. Queeg of the stage production.
10. Early Western star, also former Navy boxing champ.
11. Tootie Smith of Meet Me in St. Louis.
12. The second Tugboat Annie.
13. Dancing teenager, often with Donald O'Connor.
14. Elliott Ness of TV.
15. Child star of Kim and The Boy with Green Hair.
16. Won Supporting Actress Oscar for East of Eden.
17. Nominated for Best Actor for The Mark.
18. Female swimming star of the 1940s and 50s.
19. Beautiful Oriental mystery lady, born in Los Angeles.
20. Married Robert Wagner twice.

Scene from *This Is The Army* (1943), in which Ronald Reagan and Joan Leslie are married. George Murphy (as Reagan's father) and Charles Butterworth witness the ceremony.

More studio publicity head shots of Ronald Reagan. Circa 1940.

THE FILMS OF RONALD REAGAN

1. Love Is on the Air (WB, 1937)
2. Submarine D-1 (WB, 1937)*
3. Hollywood Hotel (WB, 1938)
4. Swing Your Lady (WB, 1938)
5. Sergeant Murphy (WB, 1938)
6. Accidents Will Happen (WB, 1938)
7. Cowboy From Brooklyn (WB, 1938)
8. Boy Meets Girl (WB, 1938)
9. Girls on Probation (WB, 1938)
10. Brother Rat (WB, 1938)
11. Going Places (WB, 1939)
12. Secret Service of the Air (Wb, 1939)
13. Dark Victory (WB, 1939)
14. Code of the Secret Service (WB, 1939)
15. Naughty but Nice (WB, 1939)
16. Hell's Kitchen (WB, 1939)
17. Angels Wash Their Faces (WB, 1939)
18. Smashing the Money Ring (WB, 1939)
19. Brother Rat and a Baby (WB, 1940)
20. An Angel from Texas (WB, 1940)
21. Murder in the Air (WB, 1940)
22. Knute-Rockne--All American (WB, 1940)
23. Tugboat Annie Sails Again (WB, 1940)
24. Santa Fe Trail (WB, 1940)
25. The Bad Man (MGM, 1941)
26. Million Dollar Baby (WB, 1941)
27. Nine Lives Are Not Enough (WB, 1941)
28. International Squadron (WB, 1941)
29. Kings Row (WB, 1942)
30. Juke Girl (WB, 1942)
31. Desperate Journey (WB, 1942)
32. This Is the Army (WB, 1943)
33. Stallion Road (WB, 1947)
34. That Hagen Girl (WB, 1947)
35. The Voice of the Turtle (WB, 1947)
36. John Loves Mary (WB, 1949)
37. Night Unto Night (WB, 1949)
38. The Girl From Jones Beach (WB, 1949)
39. It's a Great Feeling (WB, 1949)
40. The Hasty Heart (WB, 1950)
41. Louisa (Universal, 1950)
42. Storm Warning (WB, 1951)
43. Bedtime for Bonzo (Universal, 1951)
44. The Last Outpost (Paramount, 1951)
45. Hong Kong (Paramount, 1951)
46. She's Working Her Way Through College, (WB, 1952)
47. The Winning Team (WB, 1952)
48. Tropic Zone (Paramount, 1953)
49. Law and Order (Universal, 1953)
50. Prisoner of War (MGM, 1954)
51. Cattle Queen of Montana (RKO, 1954)
52. Tennessee's Partner (RKO, 1955)
53. Hellcats of the Navy (Columbia, 1957)
54. The Young Doctors (narrator: United Artists, 1961)
55. The Killers (Universal, 1964)

* Reagan's scenes deleted from final print

ONWARD–AND–UPWARD QUIZ

1. Cavalry
2. 1935
3. True
4. True
5. Chicago Cubs
6. Joy Hodges
7. Warner Bros.
8. Screen test
9. Seven years
10. He committed suicide
11. Love is on the Air
12. Eddie Foy
13. Bob Hope
14. 16
15. Jane Wyman
16. Forest Lawn
17. Louella Parsons
18. Jane Wyman
19. 1945
20. She died.

WAR YEARS QUIZ

1. Handling his son's fan mail
2. Football player
3. Adonis
4. 32 inches
5. His brother, Neil
6. Errol Flynn
7. Lew Wasserman
8. Second lieutenant
9. Contact lenses
10. Training films
11. This is the Army
12. $250 a month
13. George Murphy
14. Corporal
15. Service charities
16. C
17. A
18. B
19. Captain
20. 22

SCREEN NAMES QUIZ I

1. F
2. J
3. Q
4. O
5. G
6. A
7. K
8. S
9. B
10. H
11. L
12. C
13. P
14. D
15. M
16. T
17. R
18. N
19. E
20. I

SCREEN NAMES QUIZ II

1. F
2. K
3. P
4. T
5. A
6. G
7. L
8. S
9. B
10. M
11. H
12. N
13. C
14. Q
15. I
16. R
17. O
18. D
19. J
20. E

SCREEN PROFESSIONS QUIZ I

1. G
2. J
3. I
4. H
5. K
6. L
7. E
8. F
9. P
10. R
11. S
12. Q
13. A
14. T
15. C
16. O
17. D
18. M
19. N
20. B

SCREEN PROFESSIONS QUIZ II

1. F
2. H
3. K
4. I
5. M
6. O
7. A
8. N
9. T
10. P
11. B
12. Q
13. S
14. C
15. R
16. L
17. E
18. J
19. G
20. D

LEADING LADIES QUIZ I

1. F
2. G
3. J
4. K
5. P
6. O
7. L
8. H
9. A
10. I
11. Q
12. B
13. C
14. S
15. R
16. M
17. N
18. E
19. T
20. D

LEADING LADIES QUIZ II

1. E
2. G
3. I
4. F
5. O
6. N
7. P
8. M
9. T
10. R
11. S
12. Q
13. D
14. B
15. H
16. K
17. L
18. J
19. A
20. C

MOVIE GENRE QUIZ I

1. G
2. S
3. N
4. K
5. L
6. B
7. Q
8. J
9. A
10. F
11. E
12. H
13. C
14. T
15. M
16. O
17. P
18. I
19. R
20. D

MOVIE GENRE QUIZ II

1. E
2. K
3. M
4. N
5. L
6. A
7. D
8. J
9. T
10. B
11. I
12. P
13. O
14. Q
15. C
16. H
17. R
18. G
19. S
20. F

FILM GEOGRAPHY QUIZ

1. Cowboy from Brooklyn
2. Hong Kong
3. Kings Row
4. Tennessee's Partner
5. Cattle Queen of Montana
6. Stallion Road
7. Korea
8. England
9. Florida
10. Germany
11. The Girl from Jones Beach
12. Hollywood Hotel
13. An Angel from Texas
14. Santa Fe Trail
15. Cottonwood, Arizona
16. Puerto Barrancas
17. St. Louis Cardinals
18. Arizona
19. Burma
20. Florida

SCREEN DIRECTORS QUIZ I

1.	B	11.	C
2.	O	12.	L
3.	H	13.	D
4.	I	14.	M
5.	K	15.	T
6.	J	16.	G
7.	P	17.	E
8.	R	18.	N
9.	S	19.	F
10.	Q	20.	A

SCREEN DIRECTORS QUIZ II

1.	E	11.	Q
2.	I	12.	S
3.	G	13.	D
4.	N	14.	B
5.	J	15.	R
6.	T	16.	M
7.	O	17.	H
8.	L	18.	K
9.	P	19.	F
10.	A	20.	C

SONGS FROM RONALD REAGAN'S FILMS QUIZ

1.	C	11.	C
2.	H	12.	D
3.	E	13.	B
4.	C	14.	I
5.	D	15.	C
6.	B	16.	D
7.	C	17.	C
8.	E	18.	F
9.	D	19.	G
10.	A	20.	D

AUTHORS OF RONALD REAGAN'S FILMS QUIZ

1.	E	11.	O
2.	G	12.	R
3.	M	13.	D
4.	I	14.	J
5.	P	15.	H
6.	L	16.	T
7.	N	17.	B
8.	Q	18.	K
9.	S	19.	F
10.	A	20.	C

KINGS ROW QUIZ I

1. Sam Wood
2. Henry Bellaman
3. Casey Robinson
4. James Wong Howe
5. Erich Wolfgang Korngold
6. William Cameron Menzies
7. Drake McHugh
8. Randy Monahan
9. Parris Mitchell
10. Cassandra (Cassie) Tower
11. Douglas Croft and Scotty Beckett
12. Ann Todd and Mary Thomas
13. Charles Coburn
14. Judith Anderson
15. Claude Rains
16. Nancy Coleman
17. Karen Verne
18. Maria Ouspenskaya
19. Harry Davenport
20. Ernest Cossart

KINGS ROW QUIZ II

1. She was incurably insane, as was her mother. Also, the film hinted at an incestuous relationship.
2. An embezzlement at the bank
3. Ginny and Poppy Ross
4. Pa Monahan
5. Railroad yard foreman
6. A falling pile of boxes threw him into the path of a train.
7. Dr. Henry Gordon
8. To punish Drake for his hedonistic ways and because his daughter, Louise, was in love with Drake
9. Louise Gordon
10. Randy's brother, Tom Monahan
11. Cancer
12. Vienna
13. James Stephenson
14. He died after completing International Squadron at the age of 53.
15. Tyrone Power
16. Bette Davis and Ida Lupino
17. Dennis Morgan, Jack Carson, Jeffrey Lynn, Eddie Albert
18. "Randy, where's the rest of me?"
19. "Mary, Mother of God! Mary, Mother of God!"
20. She reminded him of Cassandra Tower.

120

SANTA FE TRAIL QUIZ

1. Michael Curtiz
2. Sol Polito
3. Max Steiner
4. George Armstrong Custer
5. Jeb Stuart
6. Raymond Massey
7. Gene Reynolds and Alan Baxter
8. Moroni Olsen
9. David Bruce
10. Erville Anderson
11. William Marshall
12. Frank Wilcox
13. George Hayward
14. Susan Peters
15. Random Harvest
16. Fort Leavenworth, Kansas
17. West Point Academy
18. Harper's Ferry, Virginia
19. Col. Robert E. Lee
20. They Died With Their Boots On

STORM WARNING QUIZ

1. Stuart Heisler
2. Warner Bros.
3. Jerry Wald
4. Daniel Fuchs and Richard Brooks
5. Milo Anderson
6. Doris Day
7. Steve Cochran
8. Factory worker
9. District attorney
10. Traveling dress model
11. Ku Klux Klan
12. A Klan murder
13. Lauren Bacall
14. So she could accompany Humphrey Bogart to Africa to film The African Queen
15. Corona
16. Black Legion
17. Humphrey Bogart
18. Ann Sheridan
19. Dick Foran and Erin O'Brien Moore
20. Archie Mayo

BROTHER RAT QUIZ

1. John Monks, Jr. and Fred F. Finkelhoffe
2. Wayne Morris
3. Eddie Albert
4. Ronald Reagan
5. Virginia Military Institute
6. Priscilla Lane
7. Jane Wyman
8. Jane Bryan
9. Baseball
10. He is secretly married, which is forbidden by the Academy.
11. She is the commandant's daughter.
12. Roman Holiday (1953) and The Heartbreak Kid (1972)
13. Margo
14. Edward Albert
15. Moroni Olsen
16. Commencement
17. Sports coach at VMI
18. On a good-will tour plane to Peru
19. Wayne Morris
20. Jane Bryan

KNUTE ROCKNE—ALL AMERICAN QUIZ

1. Lloyd Bacon
2. Tony Gaudio
3. Ray Heindorf
4. Pat O'Brien
5. George Gipp
6. The Gipper
7. Nothing-he was a Protestant
8. Notre Dame
9. Gale Page
10. Streptocus, complicated by pneumonia
11. "Let's go in and win this one for the Gipper."
12. Quarterback
13. John Qualen and Dorothy Tree
14. Johnny Sheffield
15. "Boy" in the Tarzan series
16. The Four Horsemen of Notre Dame
17. Norway
18. Phlebitis
19. In a plane crash
20. "Someday, when things are tough, maybe you can ask the boys to go in there and win just once for the Gipper."

RONALD REAGAN'S HOLLYWOOD FRIENDS QUIZ

1. Ann Sheridan
2. George Brent
3. Jack Benny
4. Mary Livingstone
5. Barbara Stanwyck
6. Robert Taylor
7. Pat and Eloise O'Brien
8. William Holden and wife, Brenda Marshall
9. James Stewart
10. Frank Sinatra
11. Dean Martin
12. Don Rickles
13. Errol Flynn
14. Olivia de Havilland
15. Lionel Barrymore
16. Dennis Morgan
17. John Payne
18. Anita Louise
19. Patricia Ellis
20. Dick Powell

RONALD REAGAN'S FRIENDS AND FILM CO-WORKERS QUIZ

1.	P	11.	J
2.	G	12.	Q
3.	E	13.	K
4.	D	14.	L
5.	M	15.	I
6.	S	16.	T
7.	N	17.	F
8.	C	18.	H
9.	R	19.	A
10.	O	20.	B

RONALD REAGAN FILM ANTONYMS QUIZ

1. The Voice of the Turtle
2. Storm Warning
3. Night unto Night
4. It's a Great Feeling
5. Dark Victory
6. The Bad Man
7. Million Dollar Baby
8. Nine Lives Are Not Enough
9. Stallion Road
10. The Last Outpost
11. The Hasty Heart
12. The Winning Team
13. The Killers
14. Love Is on the Air
15. Tropic Zone
16. Law and Order
17. Hell's Kitchen
18. Angels Wash Their Faces
19. Naughty but Nice
20. Going Places

OSCAR WINNERS AND NOMINEES IN RONALD REAGAN FILMS QUIZ I

1. Bette Davis - **Dangerous** and Jezebel
2. Maria Ouspenskaya - Dodsworth and Love Affair
3. Charles Coburn - The More the Merrier
4. Edmund Gwenn - Miracle on 34th Street
5. Olivia de Havilland - To Each His Own and The Heiress
6. Donald Crisp - How Green Was My Valley
7. Broderick Crawford - All the King's Men
8. James Stephenson - The Letter
9. Ralph Bellamy - The Awful Truth
10. Patricia Neal - Hud
11. Henry Travers - Mrs. Miniver and It's A Wonderful Life
12. Gene Lockhart - Algiers
13. Susan Hayward - I Want to Live
14. Albert Basserman - Foreign Correspondent
15. Eve Arden - Mildred Pierce and Anatomy of a Murder
16. Raymond Massey - Abe Lincoln in Illinois
17. Wallace Beery - The Champ Interchangeable
18. Lionell Barrymore - A Free Soul
19. Spring Byington - You Can't Take It with You
20. Ruth Hussey - The Philadelphia Story

OSCAR WINNERS AND NOMINEES IN RONALD REAGAN FILMS QUIZ II

1. Claude Rains - Mr. Smith Goes to Washington, Mr. Skeffington, Notorious, Casablanca
2. Oscar Homolka - I Remember Mama
3. Jane Wyman - Johnny Belinda
4. Marjorie Rambeau - Primrose Path, Torch Song
5. Barbara Stanwyck - Stella Dallas, Ball of Fire, Double Indemnity, Sorry, Wrong Number.
6. Ginger Rogers - Kitty Foyle
7. Doris Day - Pillow Talk
8. Van Heflin - Johnny Eager
9. Susan Peters - Random Harvest
10. Humphrey Bogart - The African Queen
11. Dorothy Malone - Written on the Wind
12. Judith Anderson - Rebecca
13. Marjorie Main - The Egg and I
14. Arthur Kennedy - Champion, Trial, Peyton Place , Some Came Running
15. Richard Todd - The Hasty Heart
16. Una Merkel - Summer and Smoke
17. Eleanor Parker - Caged, Detective Story, Interrupted Melody
18. Chill Wills - The Alamo
19. Eddie Albert - Roman Holiday, The Heartbreak Kid
20. James Gleason - Here Comes Mr. Jordan

NANCY DAVIS MOVIE QUIZ

1. Hellcats of the Navy
2. Navy nurse
3. Naval commander
4. World War II
5. Ann Sothern and Zachary Scott
6. The Next Voice You Hear
7. A pregnant housewife
8. Gary Gray
9. James Whitmore
10. Shadow in the Sky
11. Ralph Meeker
12. It's a Big Country
13. The Doctor and the Girl
14. East Side, West Side
15. Cyd Charisse
16. Night into Morning
17. Ray Milland and John Hodiak
18. Ray Milland
19. George Murphy
20. Donovan's Brian with Lew Ayres and Gene Evans

JANE WYMAN QUIZ I

1. Sara Jane Falkes
2. January 4, 1914
3. St. Joseph, Mo.
4. LeJerne Pechelle
5. Parisienne singer/actress
6. Noyes Grammar School, St. Joseph
7. Los Angeles High School
8. Columbia College of Missouri
9. Myron Futterman
10. January 28, 1937, in New Orleans, La.
11. December 6, 1938
12. Brother Rat
13. January 6, 1940
14. Ice-blue satin
15. Maureen Elizabeth
16. January 4, 1941
17. Michael
18. 1946
19. 1948
20. Fred Karger (twice)

JANE WYMAN QUIZ II

1. Brother Rat, Brother Rat and a Baby, An Angel from Texas, Tugboat Annie Sails Again
2. Wayne Morris and Eddie Albert
3. Priscilla Lane and Jane Bryan
4. Marjorie Rambeau and Alan Hale
5. Helen Morgan
6. Ann Blyth
7. Johnny Belinda
8. "If I had to name a corespondent, it would be Johnny Belinda."
9. The Yearling, The Blue Veil, Magnificent Obsession
10. Nursemaid
11. Dress-shop owner
12. Flight attendant
13. Deaf-mute
14. Crippled
15. Blind
16. Blind
17. Kay Kyser
18. Edward G. Robinson
19. John Payne
20. James Stewart

RONALD REAGAN "SUPPORTS" QUIZ I

1. Helmut Dantine
2. Faye Emerson
3. Louella Parsons
4. Joan Perry
5. Joan Blondell's
6. Cora Witherspoon
7. Gene Nelson
8. Reginald Denny
9. Dame Judith Anderson
10. Peggy Knudson
11. Eve Arden
12. Harry Davenport
13. Jack Carson
14. Henry Travers
15. Eddie Bracken
16. Kaaren Verne
17. Virginia Field
18. Broderick Crawford
19. Ted Donaldson
20. Olymphe Branda

RONALD REAGAN "SUPPORTS" QUIZ II

1. ZaSu Pitts
2. James Stephenson
3. Alan Hale
4. Guinn "Big Boy" Williams
5. Richard Whorf
6. The Dead End Kids
7. Billy Halop, Leo Gorcey, Gabriel Dell, Huntz Hall, Bobby Jordan, Bernard Punsley
8. The Bowery Boys
9. Gene Lockhart
10. William Lundigan
11. Arthur Kennedy
12. Champion, Trial, Peyton Place, Some Came Running
13. James Gleason
14. Lucille and Russell Gleason
15. Lee Patrick
16. Patrice Wymore
17. Edward Arnold
18. Diamond Jim and Lillian Russell
19. The Toast of New York
20. Helen Broderick

RONALD REAGAN "SUPPORTS" QUIZ III

1. Nigel Bruce
2. Dewey Martin
3. Frank Lovejoy
4. Noah Beery, Jr.
5. Alan Baxter
6. Ronald Sinclair
7. Danny Chang
8. Geraldine Fitzgerald
9. Kate Smith
10. Rosemary DeCamp
11. Zachary Scott
12. Walter Slezak
13. Lady May Lawford
14. Steve Forrest
15. Bruce Bennett
16. New Adventures of Tarzan
17. Herman Brix
18. Oscar Homolka
19. Irving Berlin
20. John Litel

RONALD REAGAN "SUPPORTS" QUIZ IV

1. Colleen Gray
2. Van Heflin
3. Gene Reynolds
4. Albert Basserman
5. Elsa Basserman
6. Charles Butterworth
7. Estralita
8. Moroni Olsen
9. Gertrude Neisen
10. Ward Bond
11. Grant Withers
12. George Tobias
13. Osa Massen
14. William Tracy
15. Dorothy Peterson
16. Marjorie Main
17. Arthur Treacher
18. Milburn Stone
19. Frances Langford
20. Frank McHugh

RONALD REAGAN "SUPPORTS" QUIZ V

1. Louise Fazenda
2. Carole Landis
3. William Marshall
4. Neil Reagan, brother
5. Tom Conway
6. Julie Bishop
7. Susan Peters
8. Howard Da Silva
9. Sig Ruman
10. Una Merkel
11. Chill Wills
12. Cliff Edwards
13. John Emery
14. Dolores Costello
15. Dick Foran
16. Penny Singleton
17. Ralph Bellamy
18. Harry Barris
19. Willie Best
20. Chris-Pin Martin

RONALD REAGAN "SUPPORTS" QUIZ VI

1. Nancy Coleman
2. Ted Healy
3. Benny Goodman and Raymond Paige
4. Margaret Hamilton
5. Maxie Rosenbloom
6. Donald Crisp
7. Allen Jenkins
8. Glenda Farrell
9. Johnny Sheffield
10. Frankie Thomas
11. John Qualen
12. Kane Richmond
13. Johnnie "Scat" Davis
14. Eddie Foy, Jr.
15. Eddie Acuff
16. Louise Beavers
17. Ruth Donnelly
18. Eduardo Ciannelli
19. Nat Pendleton
20. Charles Middleton

WAYNE MORRIS MOVIE QUIZ

1. Submarine D-1, Brother Rat, Brother Rat and a Baby, An Angel from Texas, The Voice of the Turtle, John Loves Mary
2. Twice
3. Three - one son, two daughters
4. Prize fighter
5. Naval officer
6. Pilot student
7. Newspaper reporter
8. Broadway producer
9. VMI cadet
10. Priscilla Lane
11. Four
12. Joan Blondell
13. Bette Davis
14. Jane Bryan
15. Ida Lupino
16. Jane Wyman
17. Dolores Moran
18. Pat O'Brien
19. James Cagney
20. Jane Wyman

ALAN HALE MOVIE QUIZ

1. Tugboat Annie Sails Again, Santa Fe Trail, Juke Girl, Desperate Journey, This Is the Army
2. Errol Flynn
3. Anita Louise
4. Ida Lupino
5. Barbara Stanwyck
6. Vera Zorina
7. Sonja Henie and Tyrone Power
8. Guy Kibbee
9. Aline MacMahon
10. John Beal
11. Katharine Hepburn
12. Gary Cooper
13. Marjorie Rambeau
14. Eddie Albert
15. Errol Flynn
16. Louis Hayward
17. Richard Greene, David Niven, George Sanders, William Henry
18. Helen Hayes
19. Greta Garbo
20. Warren William

DICK POWELL MOVIE QUIZ

1. Hollywood Hotel, Going Places, Cowboy from Brooklyn, Naughty but Nice
2. Joan Blondell and June Allyson
3. Four
4. Ruby Keeler
5. Seven
6. 42nd Street, Gold Diggers of 1933, Footlight Parade, Dames, Flirtation Walk, Colleen, Shipmates Forever
7. West Point Academy
8. Murder, My Sweet
9. Philip Marlowe
10. Station West
11. Mrs. Mike
12. The Tall Target
13. Happy Go Lucky and True to Life
14. Riding High
15. Dames
16. Twenty Million Sweethearts
17. 42nd Street
18. On the Avenue
19. Footlight Parade
20. Flirtation Walk

DORIS DAY MOVIE QUIZ

1. It's a Great Feeling, Storm Warning, The Winning Team
2. The Winning Team
3. Mrs. Grover Cleveland Alexander
4. Diplopia, or double-vision
5. St. Louis Cardinals
6. 1926
7. Pitcher
8. 373 games
9. Dennis Morgan and Jack Carson
10. I'll See You in My Dreams
11. Danny Thomas
12. Gus Kahn
13. Calamity Jane
14. Love Me or Leave Me
15. Ruth Etting
16. James Cagney
17. Pillow Talk
18. Rock Hudson
19. Four
20. 1960, 1962, 1963, 1964

PAT O'BRIEN MOVIE QUIZ

1. Submarine D-1, Cowboy from Brooklyn, Boy Meets Girl, Knute Rockne - All American
2. Ragtime
3. Eight
4. Here Comes the Navy
5. Devil Dogs of the Air
6. The Irish in Us
7. Ceiling Zero
8. Boy Meets Girl
9. Angels with Dirty Faces
10. The Fighting 69th
11. Torrid Zone
12. Two - Angels with Dirty Faces and The Fighting Father Dunne
13. The Boy with Green Hair
14. I've Got Your Number and Slim
15. Boy Meets Girl
16. Page Miss Glory and Bombshell
17. Cowboy from Brooklyn and Stars over Broadway
18. I Sell Anything
19. Flowing Gold
20. Oil for the Lamps of China

ANN SHERIDAN MOVIE QUIZ

1. Naughty but Nice, Angels Wash Their Faces, Juke Girl, Kings Row
2. Randy Monahan
3. Henry Bellaman
4. Nancy Coleman
5. Charles Coburn and Judith Anderson
6. "Where's the rest of me?"
7. Dick Powell
8. Nightclub singer
9. And It All Came True
10. Shine On, Harvest Moon
11. Thank Your Lucky Stars
12. Lorraine Sheldon, actress
13. Nancy Blake, authoress
14. Edward Norris, George Brent, Scott McKay
15. Jack Benny
16. Cary Grant
17. Alexis Smith and Jane Wyman
18. James Cagney
19. Errol Flynn
20. George Raft

RHONDA FLEMING MOVIE QUIZ

1. The Last Outpost, Hong Kong, Tropic Zone, Tennessee's Partner
2. Bruce Bennett
3. John Payne
4. South America
5. A banana plantation
6. Spellbound
7. Adventure Island
8. Rory Calhoun
9. Ebb Tide
10. Ray Milland and Frances Farmer
11. A Connecticut Yankee in King Arthur's Court- Bing Crosby; The Great Lover-Bob Hope
12. Donald O'Connor
13. Bob Hope
14. Jean Simmons
15. Charlton Heston
16. Stewart Granger
17. Fernando Lamas
18. John Payne
19. Glen Ford
20. Jeff Chandler

PRISCILLA LANE MOVIE QUIZ

1. Cowboy from Brooklyn
   Brother Rat,
   Brother Rat and a Baby
   Million Dollar Baby
2. Press agent to
   Dick Powell
3. Piano composer and
   player
4. VMI cadet
5. About Face
6. Gordon MacRae
7. Sabateur
8. Robert Cummings
9. Lola Lane and
   Rosemary Lane
10. Mullican
11. Leotia
12. Gale Page
13. Four Daughters, Four
    Wives, Four Mothers
14. Claude Rains
15. May Robson
16. Family orchestra
17. Cary Grant
18. Jack Benny
19. James Cagney
20. Jeffrey Lynn

EDDIE ALBERT MOVIE QUIZ

1. Brother Rat, Brother
   Rat and a Baby,
   An Angel from Texas
2. The Young Doctors
3. Roman Holiday and
   The Heartbreak Kid
4. Bing Edwards
5. Dr. Clinton Forrest, Jr.
6. Rosemary Lane (Kay
   Lemp)
7. Lola Lane (Thea Lemp)
8. Priscilla Lane (Ann
   Lemp)
9. Gale Page (Emma Lemp)
10. Frank McHugh and
    Lola Lane
11. John Garfield
12. Lupe Velez
13. Anne Shirley
14. Joan Leslie
15. F. Scott Fitzgerald and
    Sheila Grahame
16. Susan Hayward
17. Audrey Hepburn
18. Joan Fontaine
19. James Stewart
20. Gary Cooper

HUMPHREY BOGART MOVIE QUIZ

1. Swing Your Lady, Dark
   Victory, It's a Great
   Feeling
2. Four
3. Helen Mencken, Mary
   Phillips, Mayo Methot,
   Lauren Bacall
4. Two
5. Leslie Howard
6. The Petrified Forest
7. Duke Mantee
8. The Big Shot
9. Dead End
10. The African Queen
11. The Caine Mutiny
12. The Big Sleep
13. Casablanca
14. All Through the Night
15. High Sierra
16. The Oklahoma Kid
17. The Amazing Dr.
    Clitterhouse
18. Kid Galahad
19. The African Queen
20. Casablanca and
    The Caine Mutiny

JANE BRYAN MOVIE QUIZ

1. Girls on Probation,
   Brother Rat, Brother
   Rat and a Baby
2. Marked Woman and
   The Sisters
3. The Old Maid
4. Kid Galahad
5. A Slight Case of Murder
6. Confession
7. I Am Not Afraid
8. Paul Muni
9. Josephine Hutchinson
10. Eddie Albert
11. James Cagney and
    George Raft
12. William Holden and
    George Raft
13. Both were prison dramas
14. Lew Ayres, Richard
    Carlson, Tom Brown,
    Peter Lind Hayes
15. Lana Turner, Ann
    Rutherford, Anita
    Louise, Marsha Hunt,
    Mary Beth Hughes
16. Ricardo Cortez
17. June Travis
18. Sybil Jason
19. Guy Kibbee
20. Isabel Jewell, Mayo
    Methot, Lola Lane,
    Rosalind Marquis

PATRICIA NEAL MOVIE QUIZ

1. John Loves Mary,
   The Hasty Heart, It's a
   Great Feeling
2. John Loves Mary
3. Army nurse
4. Hud
5. The Subject Was Roses
6. Ruth Roman and Eleanor
   Parker
7. Roald Dahl, writer
8. Five
9. Another Part of the
   Forest
10. Regina
11. Ann Blyth
12. Lillian Hellman
13. Ayn Rand
14. Ernest Hemingway
15. Gary Cooper
16. Van Heflin
17. Dennis Morgan
18. Van Johnson
19. Jack Albertson
20. Truman Capote

RONALD REAGAN FILMS, CROSS-SECTION QUIZ I

1. Love Is on the Air
2. The Killers
3. The Young Doctors
4. They are all set in foreign countries.
5. Louisa
6. They were all based on real-life people.
7. The pictures listed were all made in color.
8. Shirley Temple in That Hagen Girl
9. They are all Westerns (of sorts).
10. Submarine
11. The Killers
12. Brother Rat and a Baby
13. Tugboat Annie
14. The Stolen Hours
15. Girls on Probation
16. The films listed were those he made for studios other than Warner Bros.
17. Hellcats of the Navy
18. The Young Doctors
19. The Killers
20. Stallion Road

RONALD REAGAN FILMS, CROSS-SECTION QUIZ II

1. The characters die.
2. Both titles contain the names of animals.
3. There is an animal in every title.
4. Horseback ride
5. Both are set in Florida.
6. Both are set in the tropics.
7. All titles contain the names of film characters.
8. All titles contain place names.
9. Hell's Kitchen and Angels Wash Their Faces
10. Kings Row and Cattle Queen of Montana
11. Cattle Queen of Montana; An Angel from Texas; Tennessee's Partner
12. Boy Meets Girl; The Girl from Jones Beach; That Hagen Girl; Juke Girl; Girls on Probation
13. All have college settings.
14. Reagan played a college professor in both.
15. Angels Wash Their Faces and An Angel from Texas
16. Reagan played a soldier in all of them .
17. Gipper's deathbed scene and the "Win one for the Gipper!" scene
18. Brother Rat
19. Submarine D-1
20. In The Last Outpost he played a cavalry officer of the Confederate States of America

RONALD REAGAN FILMS, CROSS-SECTION QUIZ III

1. The Killers
2. She's Working Her Way Through College
3. The Winning Team (1952)
4. The Bad Man (MGM 1941)
5. John Brown is hanged in Santa Fe Trail.
6. He was old enough to be Shirley Temple's father.
7. Desperate Journey
8. The Last Outpost and Cattle Queen of Montana
9. The Last Outpost
10. Alcoholism
11. England
12. They are all married.
13. A theatrical backer
14. Santa Fe Trail
15. Piper Laurie played his daughter in Louisa.
16. Russ Tamblyn played his son in The Winning Team.
17. Hell's Kitchen and Hellcats of the Navy
18. Barbara Stanwyck
19. Gunbelt and holster
20. Grover Cleveland Alexander in The Winning Team

RONALD REAGAN FILM DATES QUIZ

1.	C	11.	H
2.	Q	12.	I
3.	L	13.	P
4.	M	14.	D
5.	G	15.	R
6.	O	16.	J
7.	N	17.	T
8.	B	18.	A
9.	F	19.	E
10.	K	20.	S

CAPSULE SUMMARY QUIZ I OF RONALD REAGAN FILMS

1. International Squadron
2. That Hagen Girl
3. The Winning Team
4. Tropic Zone
5. The Voice of the Turtle
6. Stallion Road
7. Juke Girl
8. Smashing the Money Ring
9. Bedtime for Bonzo
10. The Last Outpost
11. Million Dollar Baby
12. Night unto Night
13. The Hasty Heart
14. Hellcats of the Navy
15. Desperate Journey
16. Louisa
17. Hollywood Hotel
18. Santa Fe Trail
19. Brother Rat
20. Dark Victory

CAPSULE SUMMARY QUIZ II OF RONALD REAGAN FILMS

1. Tugboat Annie Sails Again
2. It's a Great Feeling
3. Hong Kong
4. Tennessee's Partner
5. The Bad Man
6. Angels Wash Their Faces
7. Hell's Kitchen
8. Boy Meets Girl
9. John Loves Mary
10. Storm Warning
11. Knute Rockne-All American
12. She's Working Her Way Through College
13. King's Row
14. Naughty but Nice
15. The Girl from Jones Beach
16. Cattle Queen of Montana
17. Cowboy from Brooklyn
18. Sergeant Murphy
19. Law and Order
20. Prisoner of War.

RONALD REAGAN FILM COMMENTARY QUIZ

1. Brother Rat
2. Sergeant Murphy
3. Cowboy from Brooklyn
4. That Hagen Girl
5. International Squadron
6. Juke Girl
7. The Bad Man
8. Million Dollar Baby
9. Knute Rockne-All American
10. The Winning Team
11. Tropic Zone
12. Prisoner of War
13. Bedtime for Bonzo
14. Night unto Night
15. John Loves Mary
16. Kings Row
17. Dark Victory
18. Westerns

STARS BORN IN ILLINOIS QUIZ

1. Eddie Albert
2. Dorothy Malone
3. Johnny Weissmuller
4. Mary Astor
5. Howard Keel
6. Mitzi Gaynor
7. Kim Novak
8. Jason Robards
9. Jack Benny
10. June Haver
11. Robert Young
12. Gloria Swanson
13. Fred MacMurray
14. Charlton Heston
15. Mercedes McCambridge
16. Pat O'Brien
17. Robert Ryan
18. Rock Hudson
19. William Holden
20. Donald O'Connor

STARS BORN IN CALIFORNIA QUIZ I

1. Gregory Peck
2. Shirley Temple
3. Joel McCrea
4. Eve Arden
5. Fay Bainter
6. Lloyd Bridges
7. Gracie Allen
8. Leo Carrillo
9. Lon Chaney, Jr.
10. Fred Clark
11. Steve Cochran
12. Jackie Cooper
13. Buster Crabbe
14. Jeanne Crain
15. Gloria DeHaven
16. Stuart Erwin
17. Rhonda Fleming
18. Gloria Grahame
19. Farley Granger
20. Virginia Grey

STARS BORN IN CALIFORNIA QUIZ II

1. Jon Hall
2. Edgar Kennedy
3. Janet Leigh
4. Diana Lynn
5. Marilyn Monroe
6. Terry Moore
7. Wayne Morris
8. Don Murray
9. Lloyd Nolan
10. George O'Brien
11. Margaret O'Brien
12. Marjorie Rambeau
13. Peggy Ryan
14. Robert Stack
15. Dean Stockwell
16. Jo Van Fleet
17. Stuart Whitman
18. Esther Williams
19. Anna May Wong
20. Natalie Wood